D1488999

ALLEGORY AND VISION IN DANTE AND LANGLAND
(*A Comparative Study*)
by Pietro Calí, M.A.

ALLEGORY AND VISION IN DANTE AND LANGLAND

by

PIETRO CALÍ

CORK UNIVERSITY PRESS

Published 1971 by Cork University Press, University College, Cork

© Cork University Press 1971

Printed in the Republic of Ireland by the
Leinster Leader Limited, Naas, County Kildare

TO MY WIFE

. . . finites, even the human form, must, in order to satisfy the mind, be brought into connection with, and be in fact symbolical of, the infinite; and must be considered in some enduring, however shadowy and indistinct, point of view, as the vehicle or representative of moral truth.
—SAMUEL TAYLOR COLERIDGE

CONTENTS

PREFACE

This study in comparison between the *Divine Comedy* and *Piers Plowman* was submitted a few years ago to the National University of Ireland as a thesis for the Master of Arts Degree. As the title suggests it is an attempt to reach a broad and comprehensive view of possible relationships and correspondences in theme and poetic expression.

Great poets like Dante ought not, in my opinion, be admired in splendid isolation. They have nothing to lose, and perhaps something to gain, if seen in relation to other, less universally known authors of the same age. Together with more authoritative scholars I believe that Langland fits very appropriately into this comparative pattern. Such a rapprochement moreover can help increase our awareness of a medieval European tradition.

I wish to express here my deep gratitude to Professor Riobárd Breathnach of University College Cork under whose supervision this study was conducted. He first suggested the subject and introduced me to *Piers Plowman,* and subsequently in continuous discussions helped considerably in shaping this work. Without his inspiration and guidance my task would have been much harder. My sincere thanks are due also to Professor T. P. Dunning oi University College Dublin who kindly shared his scholarship and knowledge with me. The wide use of his works on the subject in the present study bears witness to this.

I am much indebted also to Professor Seán Lucy of University College Cork whose friendly and stimulating advice has been of great benefit to my endeavour. Obviously, I alone must admit responsibility for the views expressed in this book.

Finally I wish to thank the Editorial Board of Cork University Press who have kindly financed this publication. Mrs. Mary Conroy, Secretary of Cork University Press, has assisted considerably in correcting the proofs and in preparing the Index, and I am very grateful to her too.

Following the advice of the Editorial Committee of the Cork University Press I have included a rendering into modern English of the quotations from the text of *Piers Plowman*. It goes without saying that these are intended for the reader with little or no knowledge of Middle English. The translations from Dante have been taken from *Dante, the "Divine Comedy" with translation and comment* by John D. Sinclair, London 1958, and I would like to thank the author and the directors of the Bodley Head for permission to use this text.

P.C.

INTRODUCTION

In reading through the considerable body of critical literature on *Piers Plowman* we often come across the suggestion, made by many scholars, that this important Middle English poem could fittingly be compared with that other great work of the same age, the *Divine Comedy*.

Any widely-read student, in fact, who makes his acquaintance with Langland's allegorical dream-vision, will, quite spontaneously, feel inclined to establish a comparison between the two, either by pointing to broad similarities and analogies, or by engaging in a somewhat closer examination of specific and significant elements which are common to both of them. This is so true that we can consider such an approach a kind of commonplace.

Thus, in order to illustrate the first type of these approaches—that is to say, remarks of a general nature—it seems proper to quote a number of statements which are made, so to speak, *en passant*.

As far back as 1895 Ten Brink had this to say:

> Before middle life, William, like Dante, had recognized that the world was out of joint. He too looked with longing for the deliverer who should set it right; he too, with all the powers of his soul, wrestled for the knowledge of salvation, for himself as for others; he too lifted up his voice in warning and menace before the great and the mighty of the earth, before princes and priests; he too held up a mirror to the world in which it saw both its own image and the ideal to which it had grown faithless. But unlike the Italian poet, William did not attain a full and clear theory of life and hence he failed to put together what he had lived and seen, in a symmetrical, dis-

tinctly-drawn picture, with the mighty personality of the poet for its centre.[1]

In a more recent history of English literature we read:

> In the vivid delineation of scenes and the realistic painting of character the poem bears comparison with the best of medieval allegories, with the *Roman de la Rose* or the *Divine Comedy*.[2]

Here we have a sort of generalized, sketchy remark which, while repeating an established cliché, is typically tantalizing. C. S. Lewis also, in his major study on medieval allegory, cannot help mentioning Langland in connection with Dante, when he considers the nature of the English poet's "intellectual imagination" whose

> power of rendering imaginable what before was only intelligible is nowhere, not even in Dante, better examplified than in Langland's lines on the Incarnation.[3]

Another significant assertion, which will later demand fuller treatment, can be found in an outstanding essay on *Piers Plowman* by George Kane. At the close of his study he states that "compared with the *Divine Comedy*", it is

> inferior in magnitude, in sustained quality, in imagination and in the taking of pains, but superior in its human kindliness and in its sympathy with mankind.[4]

J. J. Jusserand also linked Langland with Dante:

---

1. *History of English Literature*, trans. H. M. Kennedy, London 1895, vol. I, pp. 353-4.
2. *A Literary History of England*, ed. by A. C. Baugh, London 1950, p. 247.
3. *The Allegory of Love*, Oxford 1936, p. 160.
4. In *Middle English Literature*, London 1951, p. 248.

Place him at whatever distance you will from Dante, Langland is the only poet of the century, whose mystic visions
deserve to be mentioned after the epic of the illustrious
Florentine.[5]

Echoing this opinion of the French scholar, Edward Hutton in his
Franciscans in England, declares that the "Vision of *Piers Plowman* may stand as a vision though not as poetry or work of art
beside the *Divine Comedy*".[6] And one could go on quoting from
almost all subsequent critics who have given extensive attention to
the poem, or have dealt with a particular problem or aspect of it;
from Nevill Coghill to Christopher Dawson, from H. W. Wells to
Robertson and Huppé.

   In the comparison, or better, in the attempt to find analogies
between the two epics, some scholars—R. W. Chambers and Fr.
T. P. Dunning for example—have considered some particular
doctrinal questions, such as the problem of the salvation of the
Heathen. Dealing with this point, Professor Chambers wrote a
special essay on "Long Will, Dante and the Righteous Heathen",
to prove that both poets "fall back upon a mystic interpretation of
Baptism".[7] And he devoted a full chapter of a major study to the
two "Poems of Catholicism: the *Divine Comedy* and *Piers Plowman*".[8] Both, he argues, possess the character of universality, they
are the immortal voice of a whole age and contain "a positive faith
in which mankind has for some space found shelter". Repeating
for Dante Shelley's saying that "he throws a bridge over the stream
of time", the author adds:

   ... in the way it unites different ages the *Divine Comedy*
   resembles our *Piers Plowman* whose poet has also been
   claimed as the poet of Catholicism.[9]

5. *Piers Plowman, A Contribution to the History of English Mysticism,*
London 1894, p. 13.
   6. E. Hutton, *The Franciscans in England,* London 1926, p. 183.
   7. See: *Essays and Studies by Members of the Engl. Assoc.,* IX, Oxford
1924, p. 67.
   8. In *Man's Unconquerable Mind,* London 1940, pp. 88-171.
   9. Ibid., p. 88.

And he then goes on to make comparisons between the two poets, pointing out certain similarities in their mental attitudes, especially with regard to their psychological and moral dramas and to some doctrinal problems common to both. The conclusion stresses the identity of general inspiration and purpose that is evident in their search for truth and for the salvation of man's soul.

Fr. Dunning likewise established the link between the two poems on the basis of the general purpose, obviously common to both, of moral instruction, in which the only remedy for the evils of the world can be provided by the teaching of the Church. But, whilst "Dante virtually took on himself to expound the whole range of moral theology", Langland, says Fr. Dunning, "presupposing a knowledge of what Dante painstakingly treats of in detail, confined his attention to one aspect of the moral law", that is the right use of temporal goods upset and distorted, as it is, by the sin prevalent among men, cupidity.[10] Throughout his analysis of the A Text of *Piers Plowman,* Fr. Dunning strives to "make clear the structural excellence of the poem", according to a definite plan in which, against the background of Eternity, "the *Visio* develops according to the conventional figure of the moral life of man". This "consists in the resurrection from sin, through repentance to the pursuit of Truth". Having established this, our critic remarks that, in general outline, such an arrangement is paralleled in the three parts of the *Commedia*.[11] Soon afterwards, however, he makes the suggestion that "the essential relationship of the *Visio* is with the *Purgatorio*", since both are "essentially an allegory of the human life here on earth", and disordered love forms in each, as it were, a central, leading theme throughout. Subsequently he concludes by insisting again that whereas "Dante treats of all the capital sins on the side of their material element, Langland confines himself to those in which the material element—the conversion to perishable good—predominates".[12]

Fr. Dunning's conclusions, sound and convincing as they seem

10. T. P. Dunning, *Piers Plowman, An Interpretation of the A Text,* Dublin 1937, pp. 22-3.
11. Ibid., p. 165.
12. Op. cit., p. 166.

to be, on the one hand suggest there would be ample ground for further evidence and more detailed substantiation; on the other they suffer one limitation, namely, that they are drawn from a *rapprochement* of the poems based, as regards *Piers Plowman,* only on the A Text, which forms the main object of his analysis. This, as a consequence, would exclude from such a comparison both the *Vita* of the A Text—(this, Fr. Dunning claims, "is not a continuation but a corroboration and a corollary" of the *Visio)* —and the whole B Text which, with its greater number of Passus —especially those containing *Dowel, Dobet* and *Dobest*—is considered by our critic incoherent and rather abstract-minded.[13]

Now, however valuable all the considerations we have referred to so far appear to be—and valuable they certainly are—they seem to have a twofold character. First, one cannot help finding them rather generalized (this is less true as regards Chambers' essay and Dunning's observations). Secondly, they afford the conviction that, in the field of comparative literature, it would be not only possible but also opportune to examine the actual points of contact between the two poems in a more detailed study of their structures, with a view to discerning their true relationship. No matter what conclusions one may come to, this task is something worth attempting.[14]

It would not be accurate, however, to say that a somewhat extensive analysis of such a comparative nature has nowhere been

13. Ibid., pp. 187-200, *passim.* In a later article Prof. Dunning seems to have modified these views, granting a certain consistency to the structure of B. See: "The Structure of the B Text of Piers Plowman" in *Review of English Studies,* VII, 27, Oxford 1956.

14. This for instance was suggested, long ago, by an Italian scholar, Paolo Bellezza, in a paper on "Dante and Langland" published in *Notes and Queries* (VIII, Aug. 1894, p. 81 ff.), in which he pointed out many similarities between the *Comedy* and *Piers Plowman* by means of numerous quotations of lines from both poems. These appear to be, apart altogether from various inaccuracies, rather naïve and forced, since they are intended to stress "semantic" correspondences in poetic figures only apparently identical. The same article, enlarged, appeared subsequently in *Rendiconti del Regio Istituto Lombardo di Scienze e Lettere* (Serie II, XXIX, Milano 1897), under the title: "Di Alcune Notevoli Coincidenze tra la Divina Commedia e la Visione di Pietro l'Aratore". In the main, Bellezza's only apparent merit was to bring to attention of Italian scholars the existence of the problem and to have opened up a field of discussion for further investigation. Some of his remarks, however, are useful and will be referred to later on.

attempted. In fact, many interesting and stimulating suggestions were made, late in the last century, by W. J. Courthope. No one intending to venture on research of this kind could ignore his contribution.[15] His appreciation of Langland is actually conducted side by side with close references to Dante; and he goes so far as to state that "this is the best way to appreciate the place occupied by Langland in English poetry".[16]

Such a conviction derives apparently from the general inspiration of Courthope's survey which sees the English literature of the early Renaissance closely connected with continental culture, as a voice of the European Commonwealth, which was socially and religiously homogeneous.

If we are to understand the work of Chaucer and Langland, we must first observe how the problems of the age were being dealt with by the poets of France and Italy and though Langland probably knew no modern language but his own, the analogy between the character of his thought and of Dante's is so strong as to show how general were the forces that unconsciously acted upon the imagination of individual poets, of whatever race and tongue.[17]

He further argues that

the two men find themselves face to face with the same social diseases; and the ideal remedy for these evils, which each suggests, proceeds from a similar method of imaginative reasoning.[18]

From these general considerations Courthope proceeds to a more detailed exposition of the various elements constituting "the funda-

15. W. J. Courthope, *A History of English Poetry*, London 1895, chap. VI, pp. 200-46.
16. Op. cit., p. 235.
17. Ibid., p. 160.
18. Ibid., p. 226.

mental likeness" between the *Divine Comedy* and the *Vision of Piers Plowman,* such as the encroachment of the ecclesiastical power on the civil, the necessity of collaboration between Church and State, respect for the monarchical principle, religious orthodoxy and so on. He attributes "the divergence in their ideas to a difference in the local circumstances to which the ideas had to be applied".[19] Summing up these common features, the author concludes that "Langland's conception of society is much less symmetrical and logical than Dante's, partly because it is less learned, but partly because it is more practical", the latter's being "based on the metaphysical side of Catholic Christianity", and the former's on its "ethical side", as Courthope further stresses.[20]

This, it must be agreed, is a correct and important definition of the difference in character between the two poets, leading to an understanding of their contrasting poetic personalities. But it is based on a general insight rather than on a detailed exemplification from a clear and critically cogent scrutiny of the two poems.

More significant yet, in our opinion, is Courthope's attempt to distinguish between the different use of allegory by the two writers:

> With Dante allegory is an integral part of his system of thought. Following the lead of St. Thomas Aquinas, he held that the visible universe and human society were images of the mind of God, and hence, in his system, every phenomenal object was a symbol of some form of existence in the real world of spiritual being.[21]

And again, more to the point:

> Each feature in the topography of the poem and all its dramatis personae are symbolical of some hidden truth. ... This allegorical habit is the very essence not only of Dante's thought, but also of his style: he expresses nothing directly, everything by way of metaphor, simile and allusion.[22]

19. Courthope, op. cit., p. 227.
20. Ibid., p. 233.
21. Op. cit., p. 237.

Whereas,

> in Langland allegory has nothing to do with philosophy, but
> is merely a poetical vehicle of moral thought. There is no
> poetical unity in his design beyond the person of the dreamer,
> and his machinery consists of a succession of separate and
> unconnected visions, each presenting a familiar scene of real
> life.[23]

Here one may observe at once that the perennial artistic vitality
of the *Commedia* does not depend exclusively on the symmetrical
structure of the allegorical design and the skilful realization of it,
while, on the other hand, the realistic visions of *Piers Plowman*
are less disjoined than Courthope would have us believe, even
though they may not, with their external looseness, greatly contribute to the ultimate poetical merit of the poem. However, it
must be recognized that there is much truth in all the assertions
quoted above. They are stimulating and constitute a good basis
from which a more accurate analysis might be worked out. Unfortunately the examples and quotations supplied by this critic to
prove his statements are not always convincing, since they are
rather haphazard, sometimes inaccurate and, in any case, not sufficient in number to give us a clear picture of a strong support to
the viewpoints presented by him. In a word, Courthope's comparison is most valuable and useful but not "literal" enough. This,
admittedly, could hardly be otherwise, considering the general
nature of his comparative analysis, which is contained in a short
chapter of a work of vast proportions.[24]

Now we have to ask ourselves: can any further advance be made
in comparing Dante and Langland, can we go closer in our

22. Ibid., p. 238—One could hardly accept this qualification of simile and
metaphor as depending on the allegorical nature of the *Divine Comedy*.
They are poetical and stylistic devices pertaining to the poet's genius and
can be found in other kinds of poetry.

23. Ibid., p. 238.

24. See also: S. B. James, *Back to Langland*, London 1935. If Dr. Courthope's analysis was not literal enough, Mr. James' comparison with Dante,
though more recent, is not "literary".

approach to the problem in order to see if the parallel is justified in a fuller sense? Or should we accept without reservation the completely different and rather challenging affirmation by a contemporary critic, who states, quite categorically, that "comparison with Dante will do the English poet no service; there could hardly be greater dissimilarity of endowment, scope and method".[25]

Clearly all the remarks I have previously mentioned in order to assess the *status quaestionis* weigh considerably against this last one by Professor Lawlor and indicate the necessity of examining all possible aspects of such relationship, including perhaps the diversities each poem would undoubtedly present. Professor Lawlor's downright assertion draws attention to the fundamental point which has indeed emerged from the discussion I have endeavoured to summarize: that Langland and Dante created two different poems, different in conception, execution and style. These differences may be due, also, to the different kinds of audience each poet had in mind. Any brief, facile comparison which does not first take into account these differences, "will do no service to the English poet". On the other hand, it is equally clear that Dante's outlook on life, on the structure of human society, on the means by which human society can be bettered—his concern as well as Langland's—is fundamentally the same as that of the English poet. It is also a fact that *Piers Plowman* is the only comprehensive treatment in Middle English literature of the place of man in society which can be compared with Dante from that point of view. Therefore to compare the two poems in regard to those problems to which both poets addressed themselves and in regard to the remedies they proposed should be fruitful for our better understanding of Langland's viewpoints and, more important perhaps, of the creative intention behind his work. A comparison thus motivated would *do service* to the *English poet!* And from the purely literary aspect of structure and method, it will be seen that each poem is an outstanding example of the common medieval form, the dream-allegory; therefore a comparison which is not invalidated by too close attention to details (which necessarily

25. J. Lawlor, *Piers Plowman, An Essay in Criticism*, London 1962, p. 253.

differ for the reasons given above) between the handling of this
literary form by the Italian poet and by the English must, one feels,
deepen and extend our appreciation of Langland's poetic achievement—even if such a comparison only serves to set off and highlight the distinctive characteristics of the only English poet who
treats life and man on a Dantesque scale.

On the one hand, therefore, taking into account the general
nature of each poem, its date, and its particular cultural background, one should avoid the attempt to discover and produce only
casual similarities of detail in actual lines from both works, for a
study leaning heavily on merely semantic correspondences would,
almost certainly, bear poor fruits. This is truer still if we accept
the opinion, on which all agree, that Langland had no direct
knowledge of the *Divine Comedy* nor of the Italian language.[26]
On the other hand, any conclusion cannot be based on random
generalizations but should be supported by, and inferred from,
close readings of the two poems with the purpose of evaluating
the real analogies between them, the true correspondence of ideas
and thought and eventually the different or contrasting aspects of
each poet's art.

I propose, in the following pages, to conduct a study clearly
limited to the following areas:

(i) the establishment of grounds for comparison;

26. Courthope, op. cit., p. 226. See also: Paget Toynbee, *Dante and
English Literature,* London 1909, vol. I, p. xvii, note 1; vol. II, p. 137. The
only suggestion to the contrary that I have come across was made by Konrad
Burdach in his volume *Der Dichter Des Ackermann aus Böhmen und Seine
Zeit,* Berlin 1932. On page 303 we find this statement: "Es scheint mir wohl
möglich, dass Langland irgendwie von Dantes Commedia Kenntnis gehabt
hat und sie angeregt worden ist. Das wäre noch genauer zu erforschen". This
critic shows several interesting insights in relating *Piers Plowman* to the
Comedy, especially with regard to important theological questions. But I
do not think it could be proved that there exists a direct or indirect influence
of Dante on the English poet. The author of *Piers* is more learned than was
assumed up to fifty years ago by many students. He may have known some
French Allegories, but Langland is not Chaucer. Cf. D. L. Owen, *Piers
Plowman, A Comparison with some earlier and contemporary French
Allegories,* London 1912.

(ii) the approach of each poet to the nature of evil operative in man;

(iii) the theme of repentance and regeneration;

(iv) the role in each poem of a central figure—Beatrice and Piers;

(v) the ability of each poet to relate the allegorical method effectively to vivid human experience.

As regards *Piers Plowman* the B Text will be adopted here, since by general agreement it offers the most complete version of the poem as well as a richer poetical appeal.

A comparative study such as this does not have to be concerned with actual textual problems and will, in consequence, be conducted on the assumption of single authorship, namely that the poem is the work of William Langland, according to the most recent results of *Piers Plowman* criticism.[27]

---

27. See e.g. G. Kane, *Piers Plowman, The Evidence for Authorship,* London 1965. D. C. Fowler, *Piers the Plowman, Literary Relations of the A and B Texts,* Seattle 1961, advances the view that the author was John Trevisa, without, however, establishing solid grounds to substantiate his suggestion.

CHAPTER 1

THE APPROACH TO A COMPARISON

Both the *Divine Comedy* and *Piers Plowman* have for long been the object of intense research and study aimed at not merely illustrating their poetical values but also at evaluating their structural patterns. This involves, beside the technique of composition, the nature and meaning of the allegory. The results of these inquiries have been more often than not very contradictory and present sometimes diametrically-opposed conclusions. This was inevitable and it will continue to happen, especially as regards Dante's poem on which, from the endless flow of studies and commentaries, one would hardly expect to find general agreement in the interpretation either of particular points or of the whole epic. The same can be said of Langland despite the relatively small amount of scholarship devoted to his poem.

This is an unavoidable consequence of the many obscurities which both works contain and which future scholars have the problem of clarifying and interpreting. Thus, legions of commentators, from the older to the more recent, have eagerly striven to draw aside "the beautiful veil" of the "litera" in order to bring to light the hidden sense, proposing various interpretations and trying to arrive at a unified grasp of all the allegorical truths contained in the *Commedia*. But this seems to have been a relatively vain labour. If, in fact, some agreement has been reached on the very general meaning, it has been impossible to attain certainty when considering particular images, characters, or episodes, and neither great scholarship, deep knowledge of the period nor profound study of Dante's other works have helped to solve the riddles or to go beyond mere hypotheses and conjectures.[1] Admittedly it was the

---

1. Cf. F. De Sanctis, *Storia della Letteratura Italiana,* ed. Mondadori, Milan 1961, p. 124.

poet himself who, perhaps unwittingly, gave encouragement to some over-gifted exegetes to search continually for extended meanings of his verses when he prompted his readers to follow this course:

O voi ch'avete li 'ntelletti sani,
   mirate la dottrina che d'asconde
sotto il velame de li versi strani.

(Inf., IX, 61-3)

[Ye that are of good understanding, note the teaching that is hidden under the veil of the strange lines.]

True, the formulation of theoretical principles for the moral interpretation of any work of art had been expressed by Dante himself both in the *Convivio* and the famous *Epistle to Can Grande*.[2] In so doing he had aligned himself with the traditional scholastic authorities who had fixed the principles of the fourfold method of exegesis by which the "sentence" of the text had to be evaluated through the distinction of the literal, allegorical, anagogical and tropological levels, as was customary with the Bible during the Middle Ages. Unfortunately many scholars, academic and amateur, taking too literally such an interpretative system, almost since the appearance of the *Commedia,* have felt authorized to look for hidden meanings in every page, even in every line, producing an enormously cumbrous amount of discordant interpretations which obscure rather than clarify the poem, and which very often are a grievous hindrance to the enjoyment of the poetry. Thus in turn Dante has become an apostle of nationalism, a precursor of Luther, a "holy father"; and his language a cryptogrammatic text for the explanation of which a code or a key is supplied that will reveal unsuspected views of the poet as a socialist, a freemason, and even a heretic.[3]

2. See *Conv.* II, 1; Epist. par. 7. I adopt the texts of Dante from *Le Opere di Dante Alighieri,* edited by Dr. E. Moore and P. Toynbee, Oxford 1924.
3. A survey of such distortions, occurring frequently in the history of Dante criticism, can be found in Ed. Moore, *Studies in Dante,* Second Series,

It is no wonder therefore that a sharp reaction to this kind of approach and the fantastic misunderstandings it causes should come from eminent critics who hold allegory in general responsible for this state of affairs. It was the great De Sanctis, undoubtedly the dominant figure in literary criticism during the romantic period in Italy, who denounced as false the poetics of the Middle Ages according to which poetry had to serve primarily a moral and didactic purpose and vindicated its independence from any philosophical or religious creed (art for art's sake), and finally drew a sharp line between the allegoric 'intentions' of Dante and the realization of his art, a line not merely of division but of sharp contrast:

L'allegoria, . . . allarga il mondo dantesco e insieme l'uccide, ne fa il segno o la cifra di un concetto a sè estrinseco. . . . La figura, dovendo significare non sè stessa ma un altro, non ha niente di organico e diviene un accozzamento meccanico e mostruoso, il cui significato è fuori di sè, com'è il grifone del purgatorio, l'aquila del paradiso e il Lucifero, e Dante con le sette P incise sulla fronte.[4]

[Allegory, while it enlarges Dante's world, at the same time kills it, turns it into the sign and cipher of a concept outside itself. . . . Dante's figures, having to symbolize not themselves, but something outside themselves, are unorganic, are a mechanical and monstrous mixture whose meaning is outside itself —as, for instance, the Griffin in Purgatory, the Eagle in Paradise, Lucifer, and Dante with the seven Ps engraved on his forehead.]

Oxford 1899, pp. 5-9. See also De Sanctis, op. cit., pp. 125-6. Dorothy Sayers, in the excellent introduction to her translation of the *Inferno*, refers to the theory once put forward by G. P. G. Rossetti that "the *Comedy* is nothing but an anti-Roman tract preaching in crypto-grammatic form the Manichean heresy of the Cathar and Patarene Sects". As Miss Sayers observes, "the arguments adduced for these views are scarcely such as to commend themselves to sober scholarship or critical judgement": *The Comedy of D.A., Hell,* Penguin ed. 1949, p. 24, note 2.

4. De Sanctis, op. cit., p. 113.

No one can deny both De Sanctis' deep penetration of Dante's poetry and his revelation of the poet's humanity. His work is the obligatory starting point of all subsequent criticism. Following in his footsteps Benedetto Croce, who has dominated and influenced the literary scene in Italy for the last fifty years, reached the conclusion that "allegorism" of any kind is foreign to Dante's poetry as to any other poetry.[5] Croce furthermore argues that the critic must reject it as something utterly mechanic, a "cryptography", insisting that "dove si considera l'allegoria non si considera la poesia e dove si considera la poesia non si considera l'allegoria".[6] A similar bias is seen in the commentary of another outstanding Italian scholar who, together with De Sanctis and Croce, has helped generations of students and "common readers" to understand and enjoy the eternal values of the poetry in the *Commedia*.[7]

One may ask, however, if in this search for "pure poetry", distinguished as it were from all allegorical elements, there is not the risk of splitting a poem into two or three separate compartments (presumably any doctrinal content would be relegated to the non-poetic realm too). No poet, no medieval poet—least of all Dante—would allow his work to be read in such a "compartmental" way or sanction a systematic distinction between allegory (or doctrine) and poetry—that is to say, the structural mutilation of his work. Certainly it is more satisfying a task to evaluate characters, emotions, scenes and situations by a predominantly aesthetic appraisal in order to reveal the full emotional range and the great descriptive power which characterize the poet's art. Indeed, for those who are

5. B. Croce, *La Poesia di Dante,* Bari 1948, pp. 20-4.
6. B. Croce, *Sul concetto dell'allegoria in Letteratura Ital. Storia e Testi,* ed. Ricciardi, Napoli 1951, p. 341. "Nel caso particolare di Dante", he adds, "appunto perchè Dante *è* uno dei maggiori geni poetici dell'umanità, l'allegoria è quasi sempre estrinseca, e solo rarissime volte interferisce nella poesia; e se pare che v'interferisca così di frequente, e anzi di continuo, la colpa è dei commentatori, che hanno appesantito ad allegoria quella che è alata poesia" ["In Dante's particular case, exactly because he is one of the major poetical geniuses of mankind, allegory is nearly always foreign to, and only rarely interferes with, poetry; and if it seems to interfere with it so often, even continually, the fault lies with commentators who have reduced to pedantic allegory what instead is inspired poetry"] (ibid., 341).
7. A. Momigliano, *Commento alla Divina Commedia,* Firenze 1947.

endowed with particular good taste, insight, and penetration, there is a wealth of authentic poetic "bellezze" which undoubtedly constitute the lasting appeal of the *Commedia*. By elucidating and evaluating human feelings or the splendour of a picture, the incomparable beauty of language as well as the perfect correspondence of matter and form, the aesthetic critic will always perform an essential role, and hence will make more intelligible the emotional impact which the poetry quite clearly exercises on the receptive reader.

But if we accept the importance of the moral purport of the poem, that is, the message it wants to convey, we must come to admit—unless we risk impairing our complete understanding of its meaning—that both the characters and the figures of the *Comedy* are not only endowed with intense poetical life but have at the same time, at least in the overall general import, an evident allegorical value, and fulfil an indispensable symbolic function. As an authoritative Italian critic has said : "... la figura e il figurato, non sono due cose come ha creduto anche il De Sanctis : sono tutt'uno : nella figura è presente, e lo intona di sè, anche il figurato, anche l'allegoria" ["... the figure and the figured are not two separate things, as also De Sanctis believed : they are one thing : both the figure and the allegory are present in the figure and invest it with their quality"].[8] And conversely, we may confidently assert that most, if not all, the figures that present themselves as typically and avowedly allegorical agents in the action of the poem can possess an unmistakably true poetical quality. The correctness of this assumption needs of course to be proved, and we hope it will be substantiated in the course of our analysis.

Before proceeding any further, however, we must—in so far as this problem is concerned—attempt a parallel survey of *Piers Plowman* criticism in order that we may see it in the same perspective as the *Divine Comedy;* otherwise the comparison between the two poems would be flawed. A striking similarity in controversial interpretations of the poems, in fact, occurs immediately. The standard commentary or critical essay on *Piers Plowman* will

8. F. Flora, *Storia della Letteratura Ita'.*, Milan 1947, p. 101.

inform us that the popularity enjoyed by it during the fourteenth and fifteenth centuries was almost exclusively marked by a great enthusiasm for the satiric condemnation of social and clerical abuses and that the author was regarded as a disciple or a precursor of Wyclif, a Lollard, and even as a forerunner of the religious changes which brought about the Reformation.[9] He was also called a true "socialist" of the fourteenth century, for nobody better than he understood and described the class struggles of his time.[10] Strangely, Langland was not labelled a heretic as Dante was, but though admitting his religious orthodoxy, some later critics seemingly cannot help associating him with "that family of Christian thought at once simple and mystical" from which "arose most of the sects condemned by the Church as heretical . . . Montanists, Paulicians, Waldenses, Anabaptists" and so on, to whose ideas Langland did not adhere, but with whose spirit he might have a certain affinity of mental and temperamental attitude.[11] Such interpretations were based either on biased and prejudiced views resulting from anti-Roman feeling, or on the exclusive attention given to the very strong social aspects of *Piers Plowman,* rather than on a far-fetched interpretation of its allegorical elements as had happened in the case of the *Commedia.*

As an allegorical poet, on the other hand, Langland often fared no better than Dante, and one can easily come across outright

9. See e.g. E. Salter, *Piers Plowman, An Introduction,* Oxford 1962, p. 12, where we see that the connection between Wyclif and Langland was made by R. Crowley, the man who first printed an edition of the poem in 1550.

10. Cf. P. Bellezza, *Coincidenze tra la Div. Com. e Piers Plowman,* p. 1221.

11. Courthope, op. cit., p. 234. "These sects," he further says, "all bear on their faces the evidence of their common descent from a single principle, namely to act according to their own interpretation of the letter of Christ's precepts", and consequently they "acknowledge no authority beyond the plain words of Scripture". By their rebellious attitude "they have been constantly brought into collision with constituted authority both in Church and State". Courthope, however, recognizes that "while he (Langland) had meditated, not without sympathy, on the doctrines of the Lollards and socialists of his times, he was far from approving of their practical conclusions; and he remained unmoved equally by Wyclif's views of Transubstantiation and by John Ball's sermons on social equality" (ibid., p. 235).

condemnations of his predominantly allegorical character. Isaac D'Israeli, for instance, once remarked : "A voluminous allegory is the rudest and the most unsupportable of all poetic fictions ... A genius of the highest order (Langland) alone could lead us through a single perusal of such a poem, by the charm of vivifying details, which enable us to forget the allegory altogether ...".[12] And to Whitaker our poet appears as having contrived "by his striking personifications, dark allusions, and rapid transitions, to support and animate an allegory (*the most insipid for the most part and tedious of all vehicles of instruction*) through a bulky volume".[13] Those are views that, although not formulating an explicit theoretical opposition between allegory and poetry, strongly resemble those of De Sanctis and Croce quoted above.

If then we posit the thesis that the allegoric method is not *ipso facto* hostile to genuine poetic expression, we have to try to define allegory in general, and to reveal its predominant position in medieval literature. This is by no means an easy task. Perhaps the best way to do so is to strip the notion of allegory of such common but erroneous ideas as identify it either with a mechanical process, a system of hermeneutics, a cryptography, which all alike make of allegory something of a crossword puzzle, or, on the other hand, see in it only a "vehicle of instruction", which narrows its significance to a mere didactic function. The first approach, in fact, can easily lead to an arbitrary and unauthorized interpretation of an allegorical poem, since the hidden meanings and the key which reveals them could be supplied only by the author himself. The second could, on the other hand, make of the admonitions and instructions of a poet a more or less skilful piece of unwieldly and, in the long run, tedious moralizing.

Certainly there are many medieval or even Renaissance allegories which can be said to belong to one or other of those categories. But to the truly great poets allegory is much more than a rhetorical or literary device used to express their ideas, and its implications go far beyond the purpose or the intention of admon-

12. Reported in Skeat's edition of *Piers Plowman*, Oxford 1886, under the heading "Criticism of the Poem", vol. II, p. xxxix.
13. Ibid., p. xl (italics mine).

ishing or instructing. For them allegory is principally and primarily a legitimate and even masterly *way of embodying great and supreme spiritual truths*. For the medieval poet, in particular, it is a means of visualizing the fateful, unending struggle between good and evil, the shortcomings of human nature and its worth, the relations between man and God, in a word the varied and at the same time unchanging aspects of the individual and universal Christian life. Dr. Tillyard makes the point clear: "The essential subject of medieval epic was the Christian one of the earthly pilgrimage leading to salvation and a higher life", and "However closely medieval allegory became tied up with rhetoric, however mathematical and mechanical was the medieval theory of multiple meanings, the allegorical form was not a mere accretion, but the index of a whole new way of thought".[14]

It is not that the allegorical method was absolutely indispensable in order to express religious ideas or to convey moral convictions. The poet might have said all he had to say in a direct, straightforward way, and according to the depth of his humanity or the degree of intensity of his feelings might have achieved an equal artistic excellence. But allegory, through its inherent approach in depth to its subject by means of symbolism or personification, would actually enable a poet to penetrate more profoundly into a superior world of transcendence, not just for the sake of idle contemplative speculation on its values, but in order to try to understand them and to work them into the very life of men. By doing so the poet confers on mankind the sense of a higher destiny, directing and elevating it towards a divine dignity. This does not mean, of course, that all poets would attain such a deep "insight" into a superior order of things. Everything depends on the individual ability to reach beyond the possibilities of common experiences, and to reveal in a harmonious wholeness the vision of a higher reality as well as to frame it into an artistically valid form. We can safely assume that Dante did so—and successfully. Whether Langland achieved the same result, no matter how completely or partially, we shall attempt to examine. In any case it is clear that

14. *The English Epic and its Background*, London 1954, p. 131, 134.

both poets used allegory as a vital, even indispensable part of their poetic method, and whatever artistic merits they reveal must, consequently, be intimately connected with allegory. This cannot therefore be dismissed as a merely otiose convention, but must be considered as an effective vehicle for their ethical principles and, above all, for their religious feelings. To deny this would be to reject the belief that religion is able to produce genuine poetical emotion and, therefore, true as well as great poetry.[15]

Another equally important consideration, however, must enter our discussion at this point. In recognizing the paramount importance of allegory as a basic foundation of some of the highest literature—and with this kind we necessarily have to associate both the *Divine Comedy* and *Piers Plowman*—a second mistake should be avoided, that is to assume the mode as applied with a tireless consistency by our poets, almost without any break, in every single feature or detail of their work; as if everything they say or every gesture and action of the various characters must have a second or several meanings, which can be discovered and elucidated. Some critics, probing the two poems from this preconceived and over-systematic viewpoint, really give the impression of building around the poets a kind of artificial prison from which they are not allowed to escape for one moment.[16] It cannot be denied that such investigations give occasionally much valuable help in interpreting many key passages. On the other hand, they tend inevitably, if perhaps unwillingly, to weaken the appreciation of the admirable as well as imponderable element of artistic liberty which is at the very core of poetical inspiration. Nothing, I think, will help to

15. See for this point: E. Salter, op. cit., p. 24. In connection with this problem she quotes a passage from S. Langer, *Feeling and Form* (London 1953, p. 402) which I like to reproduce for its immediacy: "When religious imagination is the dominant force in society, art is scarcely separable from it; for a great wealth of actual emotion attends religious experience, and unspoiled, unjaded minds wrestle joyfully for its objective expression, and are carried beyond the occasion that launched their efforts, to pursue the furthest possibilities they have found".

16. See e.g., D. W. Robertson and B. F. Huppé, *Piers Plowman and Scriptural Tradition,* Princeton Univ. Press 1951. Applying the fourfold method of interpretation, the authors, though searching mainly for relevant correspondences between the text of the poem and Scripture or biblical

make this point clearer than the following:

> We should beware of taking too literally what the medieval writers said about their own poetical methods. Most writers on rhetoric, classical medieval and Renaissance alike, assume that poets make a poem as a conscientious housewife makes a pudding, by following the successive directions of a recipe. And the poets may have thought they worked that way. But we know that the best of them did not; and the right way to understand the allegorical method, is to examine it in practice and not through the theories on which it was supposed to be based.[17]

This comment by Dr. Tillyard gains added importance from the fact that it occurs in a chapter where he is discussing Dante and Langland together. To follow a golden piece of advice such as this should enable us to avoid the mistake of "reading" allegory where there is none. At the same time it should support our conviction that a preconceived theory of interpretation based on the traditional four levels or planes of meaning must be, if not entirely rejected, considered too complex—I would say too "intellectual" —to be applied continually in each and all its divisions. To have

commentaries, extend the allegorical multiplicity too far and to every element. Commenting on this approach in general and specifically on their interpretation of the bread which Piers eats as "spiritual food", J. F. Goodridge remarks caustically: "presumably the spring onions are spiritual too!" (*Piers Plowman, A New Translation,* by J. F. Goodridge, Penguin ed. 1959, Introduction, p. 13). As regards Dante, an outstanding example of this kind of approach is the ambitious (and voluminous) study by another American scholar, H. F. Dunbar: *Symbolism in Medieval Thought and its Consummation in the Divine Comedy,* Yale Univ. Press, New Haven 1929. In the Introduction, page xi, we read: "According to the explanation of its author, the Commedia is *polysemous,* to be interpreted at one and the same time on different levels so closely interrelated that each is connected to the other and that all are blended into a harmonious whole". But Professor Dunbar, clearly overpassing the limits of his well-intentioned purpose, goes as far as to find, in the course of his study, no fewer than *nine* different levels of allegory, whose existence would have most certainly astonished Dante himself. In the ambit of modern Italian scholarship, a typical instance of exegesis orientated in this direction was provided by G. Pascoli (himself a poet) in two well-known books: *Sotto il Velame,* Messina 1900, and *La Mirabile Visione,* Messina 1902. Both essays are useful but rather far fetched.

17. Tillyard, op. cit., p. 139.

to distinguish at every turn the literal, allegorical, tropological and anagogical "senses" would engender too many complications, even if one had to detect them in one poem only, let alone in two poems simultaneously.

In order therefore to reduce the danger of turning an old canon of scriptural exegesis into an artificial principle of artistic creation, we have to restrict our comparative analysis to *one* pattern of allegorical interpretation which will point now to the *tropos*, now to the *anagoge* in each poem. These terms are not, after all, exclusive of each other and can coalesce into a comprehensive, highly allusive term, satisfactorily apt to reveal the moral and spiritual application emerging from the literal narratives. For, whatever Dante himself may have asserted in the *Convivio*,[18] in the *Epistle to Can Grande* he gave us the guideline which authorizes us to adopt, quite validly, this way of approaching the problem. Since the "Letter"—though dealing primarily with the *Paradiso*—bears directly on the *Commedia* as a whole, it is appropriate to quote that part of it which, being of crucial importance to the argument in question, will lend adequate support, I trust, to our standpoint:

> Ad evidentiam itaque dicendorum, sciendum est quod istius operis non est simplex sensus, immo dici potest *polysemos,* hoc est plurium sensuum; nam primus sensus est qui habetur per literam, alius est qui habetur per significata per literam. Et primus dicitur literalis, secundus vero allegoricus, *sive* moralis, *sive* anagogicus.[19]

---

18. Tractate II, chap. 1, ed. Moore-Toynbee, cit., pp. 251-3. The *Convivio* deals generally with doctrinal and philosophical questions. In this section, moreover, speaking of the three figurative senses as possible interpretations of the literal, Dante is concerned with applying the mode to the text of his *canzoni*. This he does in accordance with the "allegory of poets" as distinguished from the "allegory of theologians" which—we may infer—will be adopted instead for the *Comedy*. The "litera", at any rate, will be constantly of paramount importance, as Dante declares. See for the whole problem: C. Singleton, "Dante's Allegory" in *Speculum*, XXV, 1950, p. 78-84.

19. *Epistola X*, par. 7, ed. Moore-Toynbee, cit., p. 415.

The presence in the latter part of the text of the conjunction I have purposedly italicized, clearly blurs—or, better, eliminates— any sharp differentiation between the figurative terms and merges them, as it were, into one. That Dante's intention was, moreover, to reduce multiplicity to singleness is amply corroborated by the statement occurring in the next paragraph of the Epistle where he restricts the allegorical significance of the *Commedia* to one, and one only, no matter how wide and far-reaching:

> Est ergo subiectum totius operis, literaliter tantum accepti, status animarum post mortem simpliciter sumptus. Nam de illo et circa illum totius operis versatur processus. Si vero accipiatur opus allegorice, subiectum est homo, prout merendo et demerendo per arbitrii libertatem iustitiae praemiandi et puniendi obnoxius est.[20]

We can therefore rely on Dante for assuming that there is no necessity to employ a many-layered pattern of interpretation in order to explain the full range of the allegory, and that the reader can "contemplate" it in union with the poet in its cosmic implications and resonances.[21]

---

20. Ibid., par. 8, p. 416.

21. Between the two passages from the Epistle I have just quoted, there occurs another one which seems to contradict what we have assumed to be Dante's "intention". But I do not think it annuls the emphasis he has put on the basically two-fold pattern of meaning of the *Comedy*. It is a continuation of the first text reported above and reads as follows: "Qui modus tractandi, ut melius pateat, potest considerari in his versibus: 'In exitu Israel de Aegypto, domus Iacob de populo barbaro, facta est Iudaea sanctificatio eius, Israel potestas eius'. Nam si ad literam solam inspiciamus, significatur nobis exitus filiorum Israel de Aegypto, tempore Moysi; si ad allegoriam, nobis significatur nostra redemptio facta per Christum; si ad moralem sensum, significatur nobis conversio animae de luctu et miseria peccati ad statum gratiae; si ad anagogicum, significatur exitus animae sanctae ab huius corruptionis servitute ad aeternae gloriae libertatem. Et quamquam isti sensus mystici variis appellentur nominibus, generaliter omnes dici possunt allegorici, quum sint a literali sive historiali diversi" (par. 7, ed. cit., p. 416). By applying the full range of traditional interpretations to the Psalm, the author shows himself to be perfectly aware of the theologians' method in explaining Scripture. Yet I believe we do not betray Dante's purpose if we see in the four senses here referred to a scriptural example,

Approaching the problem, then, without prepossessions but with the flexibility it allows, we propose to examine the *Divine Comedy* and *Piers Plowman* in a comparative "study", putting them side by side as a revealing diptych where the meaning and purport of the one may be related to those of the other. In accordance with our set purpose, the main object of the present study will be to consider the structure of the two epics, that is the whole allegorical design embracing the comprehensive moral and spiritual world of each poet and their vision of life. The analysis which follows will be conducted broadly on literary lines. And although our efforts will in the main concentrate on following the various stages of what Benedetto Croce called, with a slightly, if not completely, disparaging tone, "the Theological romance"[22] of the *Commedia* in relation to *Piers,* considerations of artistic (in the sense of "aesthetic") nature will enter and integrate our discussion as far as possible.

but *moments* of an ideal progression, equivalent facets, variations on a single religious theme or process, susceptible of being unified in one wide perspective. It is evident that, in making use of the Epistle, I side with all those who accept it as the work of Dante. Its authenticity has been at various stages vigorously defended or contested on textual and logical grounds. Since the great English Dantist, Edward Moore, discussed authoritatively the problem, it has been accepted as genuine (*Studies in Dante*, II Series, Oxford 1903, pp. 284-374). See for a summary of the extensive literature on this subject: B. Nardi, "Il Punto sull'Epistola a Cangrande" in *Lectura Dantis Scaligera,* Firenze 1960, p. 31 ff.

22. *La Poesia di Dante,* Bari 1948, p. 95.

CHAPTER 2

VISIONS OF SIN

Most commentators agree in finding in the two opening cantos of
the *Divine Comedy* the general lines of the fundamental allegory
of the poem. Similarly the students of *Piers Plowman* see in the
Prologue and Passus I the basic theme or themes which are subsequently developed through the whole poem, that is the *Visio* and
the *Vita* (*Dowel, Dobet* and *Dobest*), as the two main divisions
which are distinct but intimately connected in one general great
design. A quick survey of the initial proposition in both works can
offer the starting point in the search for a possible similarity of
perspective whose lines may extend along apparently different
patterns, but may, ultimately, reveal an *essential* identity in nature,
scope and significance.

One of the commonest features of allegorical representation in
medieval literature consists in a vision which unfolds in a strange
world of imagined experience, different from that of the ordinary
reality of this world. With this convention both Dante and Langland comply, setting their visionary activity in an idealized landscape outside the commonplace, workaday life. The landscape,
however, in both poems is, at the outset, charged with a composite
symbolism which allows almost no room for decorative elements
but enlarges the scene for the representation of a drama of the
highest spiritual import. This is indicated by the first well-known
lines of *Inferno* I, which forms the Prologue to the "action" of
the *Divine Comedy*:

> Nel mezzo del cammin di nostra vita
>   mi ritrovai per una selva oscura
>   che la diritta via era smarrita.
>
> .   .   .   .

Io non so ben ridir com'io v'entrai,
   tant'era pien di sonno in su quel punto
   che le verace via abbandonai.[1]

   (Inf., 1-3; 10-13)

[In the middle of the journey of our life I came to myself within a dark wood where the straight way was lost.

. . . .

I cannot rightly tell how I entered there, I was so full of sleep at that moment when I left the true way.]

Over against this "selva selvaggia ed aspra e forte", the poet beholds a hill already "clad" in the rays of the sun "that leads men straight on every road" (l. 13-18). Heartened by the light shining on the summit he sets out to climb the hill; but three wild beasts—a gambolling leopard, a raging lion and a ravenous she-wolf—bar his way and drive him back into darkness "Là dove 'l sol tace" (l. 31-60), causing him to lose hope of making the ascent.

The first scene cannot be located, but the stage is vast. In it the poet has introduced, through the bare features of a desert land-scape, the terms of one of the central and fateful problems in the spiritual life of man. It is the realization on the part of a respon-sible human being of a moral crisis, the consciousness of a state of error and sin, while the perception of a ray of hope shining from on high prompts in him the desire and the will to rise and attempt redemption. Dante's imaginary journey is commonly placed in the Holy Week of 1300. This year was not only his thirty-fifth birthday but was also the year of the first jubilee of Christendom. The fact that the poet uses this as his date for the beginning of the vision, as most commentators agree, may well have a chronological as well as a biographical implication.[2] But the very first adjective of the first line of the *Divine Comedy*—"nostra"—makes the journey of the lonely pilgrim "our" journey here on earth and by such a collective indication the poet associates himself with all mankind;

1. All quotations from the *Divine Comedy* are made according to the *Testo Critico della Società Dantesca Italiana,* Firenze 1921.
   2. The pilgrim's own straying will be indicated as moral and intellectual errors in the repentance scenes of *Purgatorio* (cantos xxx, xxxi, xxxiii).

thus, the plight of one individual becomes the predicament of all who have gone astray, and "pien di sonno", have abandoned the "verace via".[3] The character Dante in the poem, therefore, is not only *a* man but Man who, at the middle point of his earthly pilgrimage, finds himself engaged in the most grievous problem of his existence, and, entangled in a state of misery, yearns for redemption and happiness. If he, however, relies on his own powers to advance on the way of truth and virtue in order to return to God, the powerful forces of evil hinder his progress. Commentators, old and recent, do not reach complete agreement as to what exactly the three beasts springing from the doorway of Hell (the dark forest), symbolize. They are deemed to represent Lust, Pride and Avarice, or the world, the flesh and the devil. According to the three main divisions of sin expounded by Virgil in *Inferno* XI, they might embody incontinence, violence and malice. Some interpreters instead, relying on other relevant parts of the poem, see in these symbolical beasts three powers—the Florence of 1300 with its Black and White parties, proud France and Philip the Fair, and the Roman Curia. No one can deny that the political events of his time deeply concern Dante and that the latter entities will figure prominently throughout the *Commedia*. But, lacking a more explicit indication on the part of the author, their interpretation in such precise terms seems, at this stage, too far fetched. Nevertheless, if we assume, as we must, that the three beasts embody the root of all wickedness, their detrimental influence may be taken as extending beyond the spiritual misery of the individual sinner to the moral disorder of society in general.[4] And this, besides, is made clear by the context itself: whatever the exact meaning of the leopard and the lion, the poet leaves no doubt as regards the nature of the she-

3. As C. S. Singleton pointedly remarks: "In the prologue, even though the tense is past, in so far as we might see this as 'our' journey, it takes place, as to time, in a kind of 'ever present', with Everyman as actor" ("The Commedia, Elements of Structure", *Dante's Studies*, I, Harvard Univ. Press 1954, p. 10). A most illuminating essay on the vast resonances of the poem's first line, is the recent article by S. Battaglia, "Il primo verso del poema sacro" in *Il Veltro, Rivista della Civiltà Italiana*, Roma 1961, pp. 31-40.
4. Cf. A. Gilbert, *Dante's Conception of Justice*, Duke Univ. Press, Durham, North Carolina 1925, pp. 69-70.

wolf. Here and elsewhere in the poem she is cupidity in all its attributes—the inordinate desire of earthly goods, the blinding power of riches.[5] As such she unites in herself the other two main dispositions to evil-doing and constitutes the gravest impediment to the attainment of both the salvation of man's soul, and a state of peace and justice in society. The Pilgrim, in fact, loses all hope of ascending the 'Delectable Mountain' when there comes the vision

> ... d'una lupa, che di tutte brame
> sembiava carca ne la sua magrezza,
> e molte genti fe' già viver grame:
> questa mi porse tanto di gravezza
> con la paura ch'uscia di sua vista,
> ch'io perdei la speranza de l'altezza.

(Inf., I, 49-54)

[... and of a she-wolf which appeared in its leanness to be charged with all cravings and which had already made many live in wretchedness: this last put such heaviness on me by the terror which came forth from its looks that I lost hope of the ascent.]

Only when the wolf is chased back into hell by the Greyhound, will human society be restored to a state of orderly progress both moral and material, as we learn later in the Prologue *(Inf., I, 106-11)*.

Set against this picture of an initial situation of deep spiritual relevance, the opening scene of *Piers Plowman*—a conventional setting of a dream with the fresh colours and sweet feeling of a May morning—would seem to point, at first sight, to a quite different *atmosphere* from the beginning of the *Divine Comedy*:

> In a somer seson whan soft was the sonne,
> I shope me in shroudes as I a shepe were,
> In habite as an heremite vnholy of workes,
> Went wyde in this world wondres to here.

5. See e.g.: *Purg.* XX, 10-12; *Purg.* XIX, 115 ff.; *Par.* XXVII, 121 ff.

Ac on a May mornynge on Maluerne hulles
Me byfel a ferly of fairy me thoughte.[6]

(B, Prol., 1-6)

[In a summer season when soft was the sun,
I clothed myself in coarse clothes as if I were a shepherd—
In the garb of a hermit unholy in his works—
And I went wide in the world to hear wonders.
But on a May morning on Malvern hills
A strange thing befell me—by magic it seemed.]

The qualification of the Dreamer as a hermit "vnholy of workes" does not suggest that he is in a state of grave sinfulness,[7] but rather in a condition of spiritual inadequacy; nor does the "wildernesse" into which his dream plunges him correspond to Dante's desolate "selva" "tanto amara che poco è più morte".[8] Langland's "merueilouse sweuene" however differs greatly from the dream-introductions of most contemporary poems where they had a merely ornamental function. It is a dream that affords the Dreamer the opportunity of developing an intense activity of "sothseing"—"the pass-

6. All quotations from the text of *Piers Plowman* are taken from Skeat's edition, Oxford 1886.
7. This view is maintained, for instance, by D. W. Robertson and B. Huppè: "He (the Dreamer) is in a state of sin from which he may recover only through the action of Divine Grace" (*Piers Plowman and Scriptural Tradition*, p. 35). In his review of this book Professor Dunning refutes such an interpretation as "gratuitous". Cf. *Medium Aevum*, vol. XXIV, I, 1955, p. 25. Fr. Dunning here is referring to the Dreamer's behaviour in Passus I, assumed as "sinful" by these authors. On the other hand, Morton W. Bloomfield holds the same opinion as Robertson-Huppè: "Will begins his poem by telling us that he puts on the garb of a hermit 'unholy of works', a phrase which may mean merely that as a new hermit, he is not yet holy or that he is, as a hermit, more sinful than is normal" (*Piers Plowman as a Fourteenth Century Apocalypse*, Rutgers Univ. Press 1961, p. 24).
8. It is interesting to note that early in Passus VIII the place the Dreamer wanders in is described thus:
    And thus I went wide-where walkyng myne one,
    by a wilde wildernesse and bi a wode-syde.
(ll. 62-3)
    [And thus I went wandering, walking alone,
    By a wild wilderness and by a wood side.]
where the alliteration "wilde wildernesse" corresponds exactly to Dante's "selva selvaggia" (*Inf.* I, 5).

age from the semblance of reality into reality itself".[9] Through this the seer acquires an insight into matters of highly human and, at the same time, divine truthfulness, which is clearly meant to qualify the nature and scope of the entire vision-poem.[10] The first scene, in fact, unfolding before the Dreamer is of profoundest symbolic significance :

As I bihelde in-to the est an hiegh to the sonne,
I seigh a toure on a toft trielich ymaked;
A depe dale binethe a dongeon there-inne,
With depe dyches and derke and dredful of sight.
A faire felde ful of folke fonde I there bytwene,
Of alle maner of men the mene and the riche,
Worchyng and wandryng as the worlde asketh.

(B, Prol., 13-19)

[As I looked towards the east, straight at the sun,
I saw a tower on a hillock splendidly built;
A deep dale beneath with a dungeon therein,
And with deep ditches, a place dark and dreadful to behold.
A fair field full of folk I saw there, in between,
With all manner of men, the poor and the rich,
Working and wandering as is the way of this world.]

It is a vast landscape, showing at a glance the whole human reality bounded by good and evil, Man-on-Earth moving towards salva-

9. E. Salter, *Piers Plowman, An Introduction*, Oxford 1962, p. 59.
10. In the C revision the poet actually omitted most of the lines describing the natural scenery of the dream-occasion, and put in their stead in more relevant terms what seems to be the introduction of his universal theme :

All the welthe of this worlde and the woo bothe,
Wynkyng as it were wyterly ich saw hyt,
Of tryuthe and of tricherye, of tresoun and of gyle,
Al ich saw slepynge as ich shal yow telle.

(C, Passus I, 10-13)

[All the wealth of this world and the woe as well,
As if in drowse, I assuredly saw,
Truth and treachery, treason and deceit,
All this I saw in a sleep as I intend to tell you.]
Cf. E. T. Donaldson, *Piers Plowman, The C Text and Its Poet*, Yale Univ. Press 1949, pp. 72-3.

tion or eternal perdition. Like Dante's dark wood and sun-clad hill, the Dungeon and the Tower represent the two poles marking the ultimate destiny of the human soul "watched over by God and the Devil, constantly in peril of spiritual death, in hope of spiritual life".[11] And although these two emblems will not be directly referred to in the following scenes of the poem—except in the speech of Holy Church who explains them respectively as the abode of Truth and the Castle of Care wherein the "Fader of falshed" dwells (Passus I)—their presence will be felt throughout, for Heaven and Hell are continually mentioned as the immutable terms of an eternal finality. As a recent critic has very truly remarked : "We must remember that *Piers Plowman* in all its forms deals with matters *sub specie aeternitatis* and to read it without bearing this in mind is to misread it".[12] The theme is therefore universal—it is about Man and God that we are going to be told—and this relationship between the human and the divine should offer the closest link between Langland's vision and Dante's as regards the similarity of the general argument propounded in the Prologues of both poems. Here, however, the poet concentrates his attention on the plain of "Mid-Earth", crowded with bustling humanity representing the various classes of contemporary society : rich and poor, hard-working people and idlers, nobles and merchants, knaves and jesters, worthy and—more often—unworthy religious, bishops and lawyers. Most of these people, busy about their avocations, are forgetful of those higher realities which should dominate their life. As Holy Church says later :

> "The moste partie of this poeple that passeth on this erthe,
> Haue thei worschip in this worlde thei wilne no better;
> Of other heuene then here holde thei no tale."
>
> (B, I, 7-10)
>
> ["The greater part of these people who pass their lives on this earth,
> If they have reverence there they seek nothing more;
> Of a world other than this they take no account."]

11. E. Salter, op. cit., p. 71.
12. Donaldson, op. cit., p. 80.

There are some devoted to prayer and penance "for loue of owre lorde", but the great majority are given over to "pruyde", "Glotonye", sloth and sleep, and to "Lecherye". Merchants are bent on "chaffare" and in the eyes of the world seem to thrive. But immoderate love of worldly goods affects also many in whom the activity of money-making should apparently be less natural, especially the friars who

> Preched the peple for profit of hem-seluen,
> Glosed the gospel as hem good lyked,
> For coueitise of copis construed it as thei wolde.
>
> (B, Prol., 59-61)
>
> [Preached to the people for their own profit,
> Explaining the Gospel just as they liked;
> Through greed for fine clothes they construed it as they
>   pleased.]

and the poor parish priests who ask licence of their bishops

>   at London to dwelle,
> And syngen there for symonye for siluer is swete.
>
> (ibid., 85-6)
>
>   [. . . in London to dwell
> And sing *requiems* for stipends, for silver is sweet.]

The overwhelming vice which manifestly holds sway over all the folk in the plain is coveteousness in all its forms. It reaches far up to the bishops, who concern themselves with serving the king and "his siluer telle", and even to Cardinals "atte Courte", those who wield the great power "a pope to make", but seemingly are interested exclusively in worldly affairs. The poet does not attack the latter specifically, but "leaves no doubt of his misgivings concerning them".[13]

Moral disorder not only reigns among laity and clergy but is reflected also in the social community considered as a political

---

13. Robertson-Huppè, op. cit., p. 27.

organization. Subsequently, in fact, the Dreamer witnesses a solemn scene illustrating the setting of the social contract: an angel
from above proclaims the rights and duties of the king as based on
divine order, while the principles of moral law regulating his relations with his council and his subjects are equally recalled. However, the necessity of reminding the various "estates" of their
respective obligations—even though the poet does not comment
directly on the proceedings—points to a situation of crisis in the
relationships between feudal classes. Besides, the following episode
of a mock-heroic Parliament of rats and mice enhances further the
elements of confusion and is clearly meant to show the futility of
political strife aimed at undermining the King's authority.

To complete the picture, we are shown officials of the law

> that serueden atte barre,
> Pldeden for penyes and poundes the lawe

> [who served at the Bar,
> And pleaded in the courts for pennies and pounds.]

unwilling to fulfil the obligations of their office "but money were
shewed" (B, Prol., 210-15). The comic overtones which have
marked here and there the vision of the "faire felde of folke", are
again present in the final scene where the noisy hubbub of shrill
street cries, songs and speeches resounding in an almost bawdy
atmosphere emphasizes once more the people's indulgence in bodily
pleasure. The overall purpose of the Prologue, then, is to present a
composite picture containing a situation of highly dramatic significance: the perception of man as a slave to his sinful inclinations,
and working in this world towards eternal perdition. Langland's
point of departure, therefore, coincides broadly with that of Dante
—the theme of both being characteristically the same: a spiritual
crisis in man and society beset by a universal evil—cupidity. In
literary terms, however, a difference must be noted: while in the
former the presentation of the main vices is—in the structural
foundation of the poem—incarnated, as it were, in the lively scenes
filled with the movement of a varied humanity, realistically visual-

ized, in the latter it is realized through a forceful and intense symbolism based on the traditional bestiary motif.

This difference of large expansion and conciseness in the treatment of analogous motifs will, moreover, occur in the remainder of the initial portions of the two poems, together with the addition and enlargement of side-themes on the part of Langland, that are not present in Dante—although, basically, the similarity of the general argument is maintained.

To the rescue of the lost Pilgrim as well as of the wandering Dreamer comes now the help of divine grace through the agency of authoritative guides who, against the destructive picture of evil, will instruct, point out and probe the path to redemption. It is the worthy Virgil, impersonating Human Reason at its best or, alternatively, Moral Philosophy, who comes to encourage and strengthen the faltering will of the Pilgrim, prompted by three Blessed Ladies—Beatrice, Lucia and Mary—who "care for him in the Court of Heaven" (Inf., II, 125). And it is he who, as a first step in his illuminating function, explains the nature of the she-wolf, and outlines the way to overcome her deadly power:

"A te convien tenere altro viaggio"
   rispuose poi che lagrimar mi vide,
   "se vuoi campar d'esto loco selvaggio;
ché questa bestia, per la qual tu gride,
   non lascia altrui passar per la sua via,
   ma tanto lo impedisce che l'uccide;
ed ha natura sì malvagia e ria
   che mai non empie la bramosa voglia,
   e dopo il pasto ha più fame che pria.
Molti son gli animali a cui s'ammoglia,
   e più saranno ancora, infin che il Veltro
   verrà, cha la farà morir con doglia."

(Inf., I, 91-101)

["Thou must take another road," he replied, when he saw me weeping, "if thou wouldst escape from this savage place; for this beast on account of which thou criest lets no man pass her way, but hinders them till she takes their life, and she has a

nature so vicious and malignant that her greedy appetite is
never satisfied and after food she is hungrier than before.
Many are the creatures with which she mates and there will
yet be more, until the hound comes that shall bring her to
miserable death."]

The Greyhound—adds Virgil—will chase her "through every city,
till He have put her into Hell again, from which envy first set her
loose" (ibid., 109-11). The nature of cupidity is here externalized
both in the insatiability of its craving and in its association with
all sort of other vices—an intimate link as expressed by the "wedlock" image—while at the same time, its devilish origin is revealed.
Until a hoped-for Saviour, endowed with the godly attributes of
wisdom, love and power, comes to defeat it, cupidity will go on
engendering evil and holding its sway over men. "Umile Italia"
(line 106)—allegorically universal society—shall be purged and set
again on the right moral road only through the intervention of a
heaven-sent personage who will restore order and peace both in
the religious and political sense. For the moment—continues Virgil
—the individual Christian, summoning all his intellectual and
moral faculties, must follow a different path in order to pursue
salvation for himself, and point to its achievement for his fellow-
men:

"Ond'io per lo tuo me' penso e discerno
    che tu mi segui, ed io sarò tua guida,
    e trarrotti di qui per loco eterno,
ove udirai le disperate strida,
    vedrai gli antichi spiriti dolenti,
    che la seconda morte ciascun grida;
e vederai color che son contenti
    nel foco, perché speran di venire,
    quando che sia, a le beate genti.
A le qua' poi se tu vorrai salire,
    anima fia a ciò di me più degna:
    con lei ti lascerò nel mio partire."

(*Inf.*, I, 112-23)

[―"Therefore, considering what is best for thee, I judge that thou shouldst follow me, and I shall be thy guide and lead thee hence through an eternal place where thou shalt hear the despairing shrieks of the ancient spirits in pain who each bewail the second death. Then thou shalt see those who are contented in the fire because they hope to come, whensoever it may be, to the tribes of the blest, to whom if thou wouldst then ascend there shall be a spirit fitter for that than I; with her I shall leave thee at my parting."]

The "other way" then, offered by Virgil to the Pilgrim, is the singular experience of a journey down through the abyss of Hell followed by the climbing of the mountain of Purgatory and the eventual ascent to the kingdom of Paradise. Faced with such a tremendous task, the Pilgrim's will still wavers; but when told that this is God's purpose, he ventures forward and starts his pilgrimage into the realm of the beyond, following in the footsteps of his Guide (*Inf.*, Canto II).

The poet has set before the reader in an allegorically clear design—though not, in the opinion of some critics, in a poetically impressive manner[14]—the central problems and aspirations of the human soul, outlining the whole plan of its "story"—the main stages of the "movement of the spirit", according to the commonly accepted pattern and scope of medieval literature. An authoritative interpreter of Dante sums up the meaning of the tercets just quoted, as follows: "How does man succeed in passing to the condition of happiness from that of misery? The answer to that question is given

14. A. Momigliano, e.g., holds a similar view which is shared by many. At the outset of his Commentary to the *Divine Comedy*, p. 5, he states: "... il canto I è il più incertamente concepito dell'*Inferno*. Cominciato con sicurezza, sembra voler entrare subito nel fatto; ma poi si svia nell'allegoria, nel programma e nell'intelaiatura generale del poema. Per la sua struttura composita e per il gusto allegoricamente figurativo esso è ancora troppo tiranneggiato dalla tradizione artistica medievale" ["Canto I is the least firmly conceived in the *Inferno*. Begun with firmness, it seems to want to get at once into concreteness; soon, however, it strays into allegory, into the 'program' and general frame of the poem. Owing to its composite structure and its allegorically figurative gusto (tendency) it is still too tyrannically dominated by the medieval artistic tradition"].

by the whole poem. At first the path pointed to him by reason
and grace must lead down to the depths of self-awareness and then
to the consciousness of sin in its true nature as well as in its
terrible consequences. Only then does the path lead upwards
through penance and purification first to the earthly then to the
heavenly Paradise, that is to say, to the blessedness in this life and
life eternal."[15]

Passus I of *Piers Plowman*, revealingly, contains the same basic
features. The intervention from above to illuminate the Dreamer
is carried out by Holy Church:

> A loueli ladi of lere in lynnen yclothed,
> Come down fram a castel and called me faire,
> And seide, "Sone, slepestow, sestow this poeple
> How bisi thei ben abouten the mase?"
>
> **(B, I, 3-6)**
>
> [A lady, lovely of looks, clothed in linen,
> Came down from a castle and called me gently,
> And said, "Son, are you asleep? Do you see these people,
> How busy they are, bustling about."]

With the same authority as Virgil derived from the three blessed
Ladies, the heavenly Church summons Will to his moral responsibility and helps him to understand the spiritual implications of the
Prologue scene. She does not, however, limit herself to explaining
the profound symbolism of the Tower and the Dungeon—the two
poles of man's eternal destiny—but, in the first long "sermon" of
the poem, she elaborates on the right use of temporal goods
according to "reson and kynde witte [common sense]", as well as
on moderation and temperance, and on the duty to give what is
superfluous to the poor. Money belongs to Caesar—she teaches—
not to God. Those who concern themselves too much with its
acquisition follow Wrong—the dweller in the Castle of care—

---

15. G. Scartazzini, *A Companion to Dante*, transl. A. J. Butler, London
1893, p. 452.

"He is letter of loue and lyeth hem alle,
That trusten on his tresor bitrayeth he sonnest."

(B, I, 69-70)

["He it is that thwarts love and tells lies to all;
Those who trust in his treasure he betrays first."]

Instead of trusting in worldly treasures, therefore, men should pursue Truth—the best of all treasures. With this Holy Church expands her theme, linking the element of Truth to that of Love—the surest and "rediest" way to Heaven.[16]

Against the negative vision of sinful behaviour the Dreamer is offered the positive indications of moral renewal by means of plain and comprehensive statements of faith which contain all the doctrinal elements the poem is to be built on. Essentially, if not in detail, Holy Church's instructions about Truth and Love correspond to Virgil's call to start on the high road of personal and universal betterment—the road to redemptive grace—for these instructions are addressed to Will in order to "help him out of, or at least, through the clamorous evil of men and deeds", as it has well been put by Miss Salter.[17] Besides, we must note that Holy Church's speech was prompted by the Dreamer's own entreaty:

16. The whole doctrinal *exposé* of Holy Church, containing the vast spiritual appeal and range of Langland's thought and feeling, is summed up in the well-known lines:
"Loue is leche of lyf and nexte owre lorde selue,
And also the graith gate that goth in-to hevene;
For-thi I sey as I seide ere by the textis,
Whan alle tresores ben ytryed treuthe is the beste."

(B, I, 202-5)
["Love is the leech of life. and closest to our Lord himself.
And also the right road that leads to Heaven;
Therefore I say, as I said before in connection with these texts,
When all treasures are tested, Truth is the best."]
17. Op. cit., p. 95.

Thanne I courbed on my knees and cryed hir of grace,
And preyed hir piteousely prey for my synnes,
And also kenne me kyndely on criste to bileue,
That I mighte worchen his wille that wroughte me to man;
"Teche me to no tresore but telle me this ilke,
How I may saue my soule that seynt art yholden?"

(B, I, 79-84)

[Then I fell on my knees and begged for her grace,
And piteously prayed her to pray for my sins,
And also to teach me inwardly to believe in Christ,
That I might do the will of Him who made me man;
"Direct me to no treasure, but tell me about this only—
How I may save my soul, o Lady whom men call holy."]

These words contain the "crucial question from which the action of the poem springs"[18] and in their tone echo Dante's request for help to Virgil (*Inf.*, I, 65; 88-90): they reflect the same urgency in his search for spiritual recovery.

Another element which, moreover, shows a striking analogy between the *Commedia* and *Piers Plowman*, at this point in the structural disposition of each, is the petition made by Will to the depository of truth at the beginning of Passus II:

"mercy, madame for Marie loue of heuene,
That bar that blisful barne that boughte vs on the rode,
Kenne me bi somme crafte to knowe the Fals."

(lines 2-4)

["mercy, Lady, for the love of Mary Queen of Heaven,
Who bore the blessed child that redeemed us on the cross,
Teach me in som̄ .e skilled way to know Falsehood."]

18. J. G. Goodridge, op. cit., p. 17. The centrality of the question seems somehow to be limited by Fr. Dunning who considers it as a "merely rhetorical device extremely common at the time ... designed to give the poet an opportunity of outlining further his theme" (*Piers Plowman, The A Text,* cit., p. 60). While this is true for many dialogical passages, here it is a statement essential for the successive orientation of the poem, in the B text at any rate.

to which the immediate reply is

> "Loke upon thi left half and lo where he standeth
> Bothe Fals and Fauel and here feres manye!"
>
> (ibid., 5-6)
>
> ["Look on your left side and see where he stands,
> Falsehood himself, with Flattery and their many friends!"]

Still unsanctified and—seemingly—not yet ready to grasp the absolute value of a simply expounded doctrine of salvation, but willing to proceed along its path, the Dreamer has asked to be shown the ways of falsehood. For Langland also, then, as for Dante, the preliminary step on the road to salvation is the necessary knowledge of evil, a probing of its intimate nature and consequences. Like the Pilgrim of the *Commedia,* the Dreamer of *Piers* is about to be launched into an experience of the sinful life in order to conquer it.[19]

The parallelism we have been able to establish so far between the two poems through an extensive analysis of the introductory portions, seems somehow to cease here. For, although from a general as well as from a particular viewpoint, important aspects will bear evidence of structural correspondence, the actual patterns of movement develop from now on along different lines of allegorical construction. A comparison of the three parts of the *Commedia* with the two main divisions of *Piers Plowman* will, in fact, reveal the presence in both of similar themes dealing with the conventional stages of the moral and religious life of man, such as analysis of sin, repentance, the search for truth by means of intellectual and emotional effort, supernatural revelation—all of which, we may anticipate, aim at an identical goal and finality:

19. Professor Bloomfield makes this common, traditional approach go back to the early monastic philosophy, especially to Gregory the Great's *Moralia.* He states: "The fight with sin is the most difficult of all the tasks for the Christian Pilgrim. The road of *ascesis* can be traversed only by conquering the sins; but before they can be conquered, they must be known. Although Gregory did not invent them, his map of the sins provided the chart for the good Christian throughout most of the Middle Ages" (op. cit., p. 60).

the elevation of the human creature towards God. But the approach to similar problems, and the organization of corresponding elements, clearly point to a diverse proportioning and artistic arrangement. These will ultimately bring out not only two distinct poetical personalities, but also the great variety existing in the vision of Christian life as the central motif of medieval literature.

According to the threefold pattern outlined in the Prologue the plan of the *Commedia* is carried out in a clear, systematic design with precise correspondence of form and content for which one could hardly hope to find a parallel in the structure of *Piers Plowman*. As much as one shows itself to be governed by a compact, sequential architectonics, the other seems to be organized by an apparently complex, unsystematic succession of scenes, arguments and themes, accumulated in an endless series of variations and repetitions. Ideas first simply and concisely stated are later taken up again and investigated in fuller detail, building up climactic moments through which, however, the author in the end succeeds in bringing home to the patient reader the important truths he wants to convey. This difference between a linear and a—so to speak—circular movement towards a definite goal, can be best proved by a brief analysis of the "action" in the two poems. The first stage of inquiry into the multiform aspects of human behaviour, centred on its negative side, is carried out by Dante in a distinct way in the remaining thirty-two cantos of the *Inferno,* while the similar investigation of sin is contained in the first section of Langland's poem—Passus II-VII.

Moving onward with his guide the wayfarer of the *Commedia* enters "the city of eternal woe" in order to acquire full experience of "the lost people", those who have deprived themselves of "the good of the intellect" and have thus forfeited for ever the right to attain and enjoy the end proper to man—Truth. The journey, which has such a tremendous spiritual significance, is, however, depicted with all the characteristics of a real one: from the surface of the dark wood it reaches down to the centre of the earth where stands, towering, the monstrous Lucifer, embodiment of universal evil.

The two poets reach the brim of the immense upsidedown precipice, a place where, running after a meaningless banner and stung by loathsome worms, are the cowards—those who "visser senza infamia e senza lodo" (III, 36), rejected both by Hell and Heaven. In this region of *Antinferno,* they are found mingled with the angels who were "neutral", neither for Lucifer nor for God, as suggested in the narration of Genesis.[20] Next our "explorers" come to the bank of the river Acheron, across which are ferried all those guilty of positive evil, fiercely cursing the Deity and themselves, and spurred on by divine justice to enter Hell proper. The first circle of *Limbo* then will show the unbaptized infants and the noble pagans who lived before the time of Christ, and "without hope live on desire". The Pilgrims descend lower and come to Minos—the unflinching judge of Hell, beyond whose seat the eternal storm unremittingly whirls around the shades of the carnal sinners. In the next circle are the gluttons suffering under a ceaseless storm which fills with stench the ground on which they lie, wallowing in the mire, deafened by Cerberus's barkings and rent by his fury. Then, announced by the senseless utterances of Pluto "il gran nimico"—the mythical god of riches—comes the futile joust of the hoarders and spendthrifts, rolling heavy burdens against one another with mutual recriminations. The way leads the poet and his guide down to the Stygian swamp, whose muddy waters swirl and bubble with the savagery of the wrathful and the sighs of the sullen. Ferried across the marsh by Phlegyas the two poets now reach

> ... la città ch'ha nome Dite,
> coi gravi cittadin, col grande stuolo.
>
> *(Inf.,* VIII, 68-9)
> [... the city which bears the name of Dis,
> with its grave citizens and great garrison.]

20. This category of damned—men "who were never alive"—is unknown to theologians and appears a typical Dantesque invention, expressing allegorically his magnanimous ideas about man and his duties towards society. Relegating those who betray their responsibilities to a region outside hell itself, Dante, besides showing his contempt for all "trimmers", seems to imply his preference for moral coherence, apparently even in error. Cf. Momigliano, op. cit., p. 22.

The red-glowing walls of *Dis* divide upper from nether Hell; on one side the sins of intemperance, on the other those of malice. To the perversion of appetite is added the perversion of will, and the second stage of the pilgrim's exploration will open with the vast graveyard of the heretics, to proceed downwards to the seventh circle which is guarded by the living emblem of bestial violence— the Minotaur. Here is the stream of boiling blood, submerging murderers and tyrants surrounded by Centaurs. Then follows the forlorn wood of the suicides "once men, now turned to trees" on which the Harpies roost. A step further, on a desolate sandy plain under an eternal rain of fire, are found the naked shades of blasphemers, unnatural offenders and usurers, these last with money-bags hung round their necks.

When we come next to the craggy world of Malebolge—"evil pouches"—we enter the realm of Fraud, where we are shown the depraved faculty of intelligence turned to all sorts of deceits and traffickings. On the trenches of Malebolge the poets are landed by the monster Geryon, the foul image of fraud,

> che passa i monti e rompe i muri e l'armi;
> ecco colei che tutto il mondo appuzza!
>
> *(Inf.,* XVII, 2-3)
>
> [that passes mountains and breaks through walls and arms!
> Lo, he that infects all the world!]

And in a rapid crescendo of evil-doing we go through the ten sections of this eighth circle of Hell where, however repulsively, we are put in contact with panders, seducers, flatterers, simoniacs, sorcerers, "barrators", hypocrites, thieves, fraudulent counsellors and sowers of discord, falsifiers—all immersed in a restless flux of loathsome diseases, horrible distortions and grisly caricature. We reach at last the "fondo d'ogni reo" (XXXI, 102)—the frozen lake of Cocytus, where all degrees of treachery are punished, the ultimate perversion of the mind being shown in the uttermost manifestations of hatred and cruelty. The significant image chosen to show this state is frozen immobility, the annulling of all life; and its incarnated symbol is Satan himself—an enormous mass of impotent and dumb matter, to which only one movement is granted : the endless gnawing of the greatest traitors of history, Judas, Brutus and Cassius.

We have travelled a long way, seen all manifestations of sin, learnt that its wages are grief, torment and destruction and with Dante are able again to rise "a riveder le stelle".

This bare outline of the first stage of Dante's journey clearly does not do full justice to the wealth of detail of both scenery and argument—nor have we mentioned the highly dramatic scenes which enliven the vast stage of Hell or the great characters who animate nearly every canto. But it may help us to discern the rigorous approach which governs the structure of the first canticle and which will, one can anticipate, be maintained in the arrangement of the other two parts of the poem. Thus the anatomy of wrongness, worked out through ten shrinking circles, containing in their divisions and subdivisions an astonishing variety of penalties, can be reduced under three main headings—Incontinence, Violence and Fraud. These allow the poet to cover the full range of human perversion. And it is the author himself who, lest the reader should fail to appreciate this, supplies the sound theological and philosophical justifications of such an arrangement.[21]

Now what elements—it may be asked—could be found in Langland's poem which would permit even a loose comparison with the investigation of evil as pictured in Dante's *Inferno*? It is quite obvious, even to those who have a cursory acquaintance with the contents of the *Visio*, that both the narrative and the structure of Passus II-VII offer an altogether different picture. Yet certain features of this section deserve to be sorted out in order to establish a significant, though limited, degree of analogy from the allegorical point of view. A short summary of the "story", however inadequate and incomplete, can help us better to reveal similarities and to stress differences.

21. See *Inf.*, canto XI. Here Virgil refers explicitly to Aristotle's *Ethica.* Commentators see in this also some derivation from Cicero and St. Thomas Aquinas, by whom Dante must have been guided in adding to the above divisions the faults of Unbelief (Limbo) and Misbelief (Heretics). Note that the traditional order of the Seven Capital Sins is not present in Hell. It will be found in Purgatory.

The "Prologue" had shown the contemporary world for the
greater part immersed inordinately in temporal cares, while in
Passus I Holy Church had explicitly revealed the purpose of
human existence, placing it in relation to Eternity in terms of
Truth and Love and their opposites—Falseness and Cupidity. But
this was, in the main, a declaration of clear doctrine. Now it must
be seen and experienced more directly. Thus, to the Dreamer who
has asked to be shown "the Fals", Holy Church unfolds the vision
of the ruling vices of Church and Society, the corruption of the
world, centred upon the all-pervading presence of cupidity. This
appears as

> a womman, wortheli yclothed,
> Purfiled with pelure the finest upon erthe,
> Y-crounede with a corone the king hath no better.
>
> (B, II, 8-10)
>
> [a woman, richly dressed,
> With fringes of fur, the finest upon earth,
> And crowned with a crown—the king has no better.]

She is adorned with all sorts of gems and the Dreamer "rauyssed
by hire arraye", is told the truth about her nature:

> "That is Mede the mayde," quod she, "hath noyed me ful oft,
> And ylakked my lemman that Lewte is hoten,
> And bilowen hire to lordes that lawes han to kepe.
> In the popis paleys she is pryue as my-self,
> But sotheness wolde nought so for she is a bastarde."
>
> (ibid., 19-24)
>
> ["That is Meed the Maiden", she said, "who has vexed me
>   very often,
> And slandered my lover that is called Loyalty,
> And denounced him to the lords whose care is the keeping of
>   the laws.
> In the pope's palace she is as fully at home as myself,
> But Truth would not have it so, for she is a bastard."]

Her father is Falsehood—adds Holy Church—and to emphasize more unmistakably her identity, the relationship of origin is now turned to one of intimate, almost incestuous, association—with the proposed marriage of Mede to the same "Fals Fikeltonge".[22] The wedding is arranged; a vast assembly of men of every rank gathers to witness the unlawful match brought about by Liar in collusion with "Fauel", and assented to by Simony and "Cyuile". Guile "with his gret othes" (ibid., 69) has provided a Charter and the reading of it provides a brilliant introduction to the following "action" of Lady Meed. The whole range of the capital sins is bestowed on the betrothed, and the "feoffment" of the rich assets is properly sealed by the authority of Hell. However, before the union is consummated, Theology rises to object to it on the ground that, theoretically, Meed could and should be considered as a legitimate means to acquire the earthly goods necessary to life; in order to prevent their abuse and prostitution the whole party is directed to London where Meed must stand trial. Although isolated from her retinue of formidable rogues, temporarily chased by Dread—False, Guile and Liar readily find employment with various trades and confraternities—Lady Meed is well able to put her powerful influence to work inside Westminster. With irresistible liberality she distributes her gifts among judges, clerks and counsellors; all the officials of the king's court are corrupted by Lucre:

> They that wonyeth in Westmynstre worschipped hir alle;
>
> .   .   .   .
>
> Mildeliche Mede thanne mercyed hem alle
> Of theire gret goodnesse and gaf hem vchone
> Coupes of clene golde and coppis of siluer,
> Rynges with rubies and ricchesses manye,
> The leste man of here meyne a motoun of golde.
>
> (B, III, 12; 20-24)
>
> [All those who reside at Westminster gave her honour;
>
> .   .   .   .

---

22. In the A text Meed's Father is given as "Wrong", while in C he is said to be "Fauel". Fr. Dunning properly identifies him with the Devil. Cf. op. cit., p. 76.

In a mild manner Meed then gave thanks to them all
For their great goodness, and gave each one of them
Bowls of pure gold and cups made of silver,
Rings set with rubies and many rich gifts,
To the humblest man of her retinue she gave a gold coin.]

But it is not only man-made law that is threatened with destruction: Meed's attempt to spread corruption extends to God-given law, too, as "shamelees" she kneels in front of and is absolved by a Friar-confessor who is easily bribed by the promise of her favours for the order—not without having assured her of his leniency for people's lechery. Ready as she was to marry False, Meed now is, however, most willing to comply with the King's proposal and take Conscience as her legitimate husband: if she had her own way she would promptly corrupt the only safe and innate principle of morality. But Conscience, who must by definition distinguish between wrong and right, breaks out into a devastating harangue, and exposes pitilessly her true nature:

Quod Conscience to the kynge "Cryst it me forbede!
Ar I wedde suche a wyf wo me betyde!
For she is frele of hir feith fykel of here speche,
And maketh men mysdo many score tymes;
Truste of hire tresore treieth ful manye.
(B, III, 119-23)
And hath apoysounde popis and peired holicherche;
. . . .
For clergye and couetise she coupleth togideres."
(ibid., 127; 164)
[Conscience said to the king "Christ forbid it!
Before I wed such a wife may woe betide me!
She is frail in her faith, fickle in her speech,
And makes men sin many scores of times;
Trust in her treasure betrays very many.
And she has poisoned popes, and injured Holy Church.
. . . .
For the learned and avarice she hasps together."]

The list of Meed's misdeeds is truly long and exhaustive; yet the resources of evil are apparently inexhaustible, and the Maiden's defence is a masterly self-justification, full of clever sophistry by which she almost succeeds in turning the tide and winning again for herself the king's favour. It becomes a king—she pleads—to reward those who serve him; servants and labourers are paid their wages, minstrels get their gifts, priests their mass-pennies: meed is indeed a necessity of life. Besides, she would have helped King Edward to gain his reward with the acquisition of the rich realm of France, if it hadn't been for the flimsy reasons given him by an overscrupulous Conscience. The retort of Conscience is, however, effectively directed towards revealing further what Meed really represents, and at the same time at reaching beyond the mere considerations of human reward and compensation to the level of divine Law:

> "Nay", quod Conscience to the kynge and kneled to the erthe,
> "There aren two manere of medes my lorde, with yowre leue.
> That one, god of his grace graunteth in his blisse
> To tho that wel worchen whil thei ben here."

(B, III, 229-32)

> ["No," said Conscience to the king, and kneeled on the earth,
> "There are two kinds of meed, with your leave, my Lord,
>   I declare.
> One, God, of his grace, grants in his heaven
> To those who do good deeds while they are here."]

The other is a

> mede measurelees that maistres desireth;
> To meyntene mysdoers mede thei take;
> And there-of seith the sauter in a salmes ende,
>   *In quorum manibus iniquitates sunt, dextera eorum repleta est muneribus;*

(ibid., 244-47)

> [a measureless meed that masters desire;
> To maintain misdoers they accept bribes;

And of them the Psalter says at the end of a psalm
In whose hands there is wickedness:
and their right hand is full of gifts.]

This is bribery and usury; those who practise it shall pay a bitter price: eternal damnation. Instead, what men get for their honest work is the rightful wage—a "mesurable hire" which has nothing to do with dishonest lucre. Conscience's argument is further reinforced by the example of Saul driven by his covetousness to spare the city of Amalec and punished by the Lord for disobeying His command:

Such a myschief mede made Saul the kynge to haue
That god hated hym for euere and alle his eyres after.

(B, III, 275-6)

[Such misfortune Meed caused king Saul to suffer
That God hated him for ever and all his heirs after him.]

Lady Meed's defence now seems to be on the verge of collapse, and Conscience concludes with an eloquent prophecy of millennial renewal—men and society delivered eventually from all mercenary motivation:

"I Conscience knowe this for kynde witt me it taughte
That resoun shal regne and rewmes gouerne;

.   .   .   .

And one cristene kynge kepen hem alle.
Shal na more Mede be maistre, as she is nouthe,
Ac loue and lowenesse and lewte togederes,
Thise shul be maistres on molde treuthe to saue."

(B, III, 282-3; 287-90)

["I, Conscience, know this, for Kind Wit taught me it
That Reason shall reign and rule over realms;

.   .   .   .

And one Christian king shall rule over them all.
Meed shall no more be master, as she is now,
But Love and Meekness, and Fidelity, all together
Shall be the masters on earth in the saving of Truth."]

Yet our only too human king does not appear fully convinced of Meed's basic turpitude, no matter how forceful Conscience's arguments have been, and he would try still to reconcile the irreconcilable. Only the intervention of Reason will put an end to all evasion of the exigences of moral law and reaffirm the indispensable rule of justice.[23] There arises a test case for the king's judgement. A man named Peace comes to the court to present a petition against Wrong, at whose hands he has suffered an appalling series of brutal injuries. But before justice can take its course, there is still another attempt to thwart its working as "Wisdome and sire Waryn the witty" come to help Wrong and try to bribe the king in order to secure his release. They are unsuccessful. But Meed, undaunted, moves in again:

> And thanne gan Mede to mengen here and mercy she bisought
> And profred Pees a present al of pure golde ...
>
> (B, IV, 94-5)
>
> [Then Meed began to reflect and besought mercy,
> And proffered Peace a gift made of pure gold ...]

The plaintiff is thus silenced, and under the appearance of legality true justice is dealt another deadly blow through venality. One of the characteristics of evil, however, is to over-reach itself, and thus provoke its own defeat. Meed's last action of corruption is so flagrant that Reason intervenes to disgrace her, proclaiming solemnly:

> For *nullum malum* the man mette with *impunitum*
> And badde *nullum bonum* be *irremuneratum*.
>
> (B, IV, 143-4)

23. Fr. Dunning explains very well the relationship between Conscience and Reason, this latter meaning "the exercise of the practical reason in passing judgement in given circumstances—Conscience in the strict sense". "Both are aspects of one and the same faculty, namely the intellect in so far as it is directed towards the moral aspects of action." See op. cit., pp. 99-101.

[For a man named *Nullum malum* met with *Impunitum*
And bade *Nullum bonum* be *irremuneratum*.]24

It is the firm, unquestionable affirmation of an absolute principle, indispensable in this context for the right ordering of the State, and the king, fully acknowledging it, resolves to rule for ever with the assistance of Reason and Conscience.

It is opportune at this point to pause for a moment and consider in what way we can relate the parts of *Piers Plowman* and of the *Commedia* so far summed up. From the point of view of structure, I believe that Passus II-IV (containing the Vision of Meed) can be said to correspond, partly at least, to the Inferno. On the face of it, the narratives—as seen above—seem to have very little, almost nothing in common. Essentially, however, both at the literal and allegorical level, the two sections are a probing into the evil ways of men, an investigation of sin presented to and almost experienced by Pilgrim and Dreamer alike. We must admit then, although in general terms, a similarity of theme. But whereas Dante's vision comprises all manifestations of the sinful life, organically presented in its multifarious instances, that of Langland is centered upon one main vice, namely Cupidity. Nevertheless for the Italian poet also this is the *radix omnium malorum*. It was embodied in the ugly, terrifying and implacable image of a ravenous she-wolf, stigmatized as being of hellish origin and categorically condemned at the outset as the most deadly evil whose power plagues mankind, hindering its eternal salvation, as well as being the greatest obstacle to the achievement of temporal happiness, as clearly implied in *Inf.*, I, 49-54.25 Fundamentally the meaning and implication of the episode of Lady Meed are the same, although the

24. Skeat (*Piers Plowman*, vol. II, p. 59) notes in this respect: "This is merely a way of introducing the words in italics. The quotation is taken from the following: 'Ipse est iudex iustus ... qui nullum malum praeterit impunitum, nullum bonum irremuneratum' ['He only is the just judge ... who leaves no evil unpunished, no good unrewarded'] Innocent III's *De Contemptu Mundi*, lib. iii, cap. 15."
25. Quoted above p. 34.

English Visionary has caught up that alluring force of greed which dominates most men, in a vividly humanized personification, elaborated at length in three Passus which deal predominantly with its unendingly perversive influence and power. Langland's character of Meed the Maiden, who pours out her gold florins everywhere and to everybody, defeating all virtues in blinded people, appears as a more original figure in comparison with Dante's allegorical beast.

Characteristically, from the very beginning the English poet has been at pains to determine unmistakably, by the revelation of Holy Church, the true nature of Meed, unfolding, as it were, her identity-card in which she is qualified as the Daughter of Falsehood, that is of the Devil—just as Virgil had declared the provenance of the she-wolf to be

... Inferno, là onde invidia prima dipartilla.

(Inf., I, 111)

[... Hell, whence envy first let her loose.]

Similarly the bond of wedlock between Meed and "Fals" parallels the image of the she-wolf mating with many other animals (ibid., 100). Before, however, bringing about in unequivocal terms Cupidity's downfall and condemnation, the author of *Piers* endeavours to witness the actual workings of *Cupiditas* in the midst of contemporary society, displaying in full the enormous driving force of the pecuniary motive. This—he wants to convey more explicitly than Dante—can not only corrupt individual consciences and thus jeopardise men's spiritual welfare, but can upset as well the orderly relationships—based on Justice—between social classes and citizens. At the same time, by introducing in the concept of Meed the notion of legitimate reward besides that of dishonest gain, Langland succeeds, through the lively but long-winded debates in Meed's defence, in dramatizing brilliantly what we may call the dialectic of money and in exposing the fallacious arguments by which men are always ready to proffer a strong excuse for their misdoings. Thus he manages to give both Dreamer and reader a

sharp insight into a central aspect of the *condition humaine*.[26]
In a certain way then, one would not be far from the truth in
stating that the *Vision of Meed* contains, in a different allegorical
configuration, an enlarged elaboration—an actualization in all
directions of the full potentialities inherent in the Dantean symbol
of Greed. Not that there are no more references to it in the course
of the ensuing vision of sin represented in the *Inferno*. In fact, it is
persistently recalled in close association with many examples of
wickedness in the realm of the damned, and not only there, for it
will constitute the obsessive incubus haunting Dante throughout
the whole poem—just as it forms the continuous undercurrent
motif of *Piers Plowman* from beginning to end. When, for instance,
Dante meets amongst the Gluttonous his fellow-citizen Ciacco
"the Hog", the sinner's greed prompts him to recall the Florentines' greed. Inquiring from Ciacco what is the cause of the
citizens' discord, Dante learns that

> Superbia, invidia e avarizia sono
> le tre faville ch'ànno i cuori accesi.[27]

> *(Inf.,* VI, 74-5)

> [Pride, envy and avarice are the three sparks that have set
> these hearts on fire.]

Or when, more directly, we assist at the heavy but useless, Sisy-
phus-like toil of the Hoarders and Spendthrifts—a perfect image
which shows, allegorically, the state of men labouring in life for
empty treasures—we realize how innumerable is the throng of
Cupidity's victims. This circle is filled with a far larger crowd than
any other part of Hell, according to the poet's sad remark:

26. In this respect Professor Kane very pointedly writes: "He (Langland)
will sometimes deliberately appear to support the preposterous, as in the
marriage settlement of Lady Meed, or put all his skill into an argument
that he abhors in order to expose both its sophistry and the nature of those
who use it" (op. cit., p. 231).
27. This relationship was pointed out, for instance, by J. H. Whitfield in
his *Dante and Virgil,* Oxford 1948, p. 34.

Qui vidi gente più ch'altrove troppa . . .[28]

(Inf., VII, 25)

[Here I saw far more people than elsewhere . . .]

The most eloquent demonstration of the strict link between avarice
and other manifestations of evil-doing is given by the almost
forceful recollection of it at the approach to Phlegeton, the river
of boiling blood, where the Violent are punished:

Ma ficca li occhi a valle; ché s'approccia

    la riviera del sangue in la qual bolle

    qual di violenza in altrui noccia.

O cieca cupidigia, e ira folle,

    che sì ci sproni ne la vita corta,

    e nell'eterna poi sì mal c'immolle!

(Inf., XII, 46-51)

[But fix thine eyes below, for the river of blood draws near in
which are boiling those that by violence do injury to others.
O blind covetousness and foolish anger, which in the brief life
so goad us and then, in the eternal, steeps us in such misery!]

We can refer also to the beastly portrayal of the usurers in Canto
XVI (lines 46-57), flapping with their hands (like "dogs snatching
at flies") against the rain of fire—those hands which should have
engaged in honest toil, but were kept inert, while their eyes are
fixedly "feeding" on the purses hanging from their necks. Look at
them in order to realize how the craving for sterile money has
driven them to that materialism which denies the order of nature

28. In one of the soundest commentaries on the poem, this line is anno-
ated as follows: "La lupa invero fa preda più delle altre fiere; e similmente
il lupo Pluto, rispetto a Cerbero" ["The shewolf makes indeed more prey
than the other beasts; and similarly Pluto the wolf in comparison with
Cerberus"] *La Div. Comm. commentata da L. Pietrobono,* Torino 1956,
p. 78. For other direct reference to the she-wolf-Cupidity motif, see e.g.
Purg. XX, 10-15, and *Par.* XXVIII, 121-3. Many more instances could of
course be found throughout the *Comedy.*

and the dignity of human labour established by God.[29] This motif is prominent also in *Piers Plowman*.[30]

But it is especially in Malebolge—the foul-smelling realm of corrupted humanity—that we see how Cupidity gives rise, directly or indirectly, to the evil perpetrated on earth and here punished by disgusting penalties. The association of greed with malicious fraud appears most evident, particularly from the description of Panders, Simonists, Barrators, Thieves and Falsifiers. It would take too long to examine in detail each of these pictures of evil. On the other hand, it must be observed that, by populating this section of the lower *Inferno* with fraudulent sinners, Dante was able to develop his views of man as citizen and of the social order itself, although from a negative standpoint. The sinners of Malebolge were not merely vicious in themselves, but guilty of dragging down all human nature by upsetting the public order, by debasing and destroying every social relationship, personal and public. From the first "evil pouch" to the last we are shown the images of corruption in the earthly City, the abuse and degeneration of ecclesiastical and civil office—a Christian society progressively disintegrating until it accomplishes its own undoing. The eloquent symbolism of this uttermost corruption is offered by Dante in the last *bolgia* of the Falsifiers, especially in the episode of Mastro Adamo, the counterfeiter of the gold florin:

> Io vidi un, fatto a guisa di leuto,
>> pur ch'egli avesse avuta l'anguinaia
>> tronca dall'altro che l'uomo ha forcuto.

> *(Inf., XXX, 49-51)*

> [I saw one shaped like a lute, if only he had been cut short at the groin from the part where a man is forked.]

The "heavy dropsy" which disfigures his body is both the external index of his own inner adulteration and the means by which Divine Justice has fixed for ever the quality as well as the punishment of typically "social" crime:

---

29. These are sinners against Nature and Art, according to the classification anticipated by Virgil in Canto XI.

30. See especially Passus VI and VII.

La rigida giustizia che mi fruga,
    tragge cagion del loco ov'io peccai,
    a metter più li miei sospiri in fuga.
Ivi è Romena, là dov'io falsai
    la lega suggellata del Battista;
    perch'io il corpo su arso lasciai.

(ibid., 70-76)

[The unbending justice which searches me takes occasion from
the place where I sinned to make my sighs come faster; there
is Romena, where I falsified the currency stamped with the
Baptist and for that left above my body burnt.]

"The deformed and helpless minds and bodies of the falsifiers—
remarks a student of Dante—are symbols not merely of their own
state, but of the state of human society that results from falsehood.
The crippling of the social life of man which these sinners have
brought about is retorted on themselves."[31] Now, I think all this
is the more interesting from our point of view, since I believe that
the picture offered in this VIIIth circle of Dante's Hell compares
fittingly with the episode of Meed's Betrothal and Trial in Langland's *Visio*. It is, of course, only a correspondence, in thematic
structure, of a main idea, equally central to both poems: the idea
being that the problem of evil is focused on the most pervasive
vice—*Cupiditas*. This, no matter how different the actual presentation of it by each, constitutes for Dante and Langland a kind of
second original sin responsible for the destruction of all moral
values in the great majority of men and, consequently, in the community. As such it not only endangers the spiritual life, but un-
chaining, as it were, every evil human impulse, represents the
gravest offence against Justice as well as being the negation of
Love. The violation of Justice together with rejection of Love is
bound to cause the spiritual ruin of individual men as well as the
disruption of corporate Society. This is the *lesson* both Dante and
Langland want to bring home to the reader, and in this, therefore,
lies the overall significance of the allegorical representation of sin
contained in the *Inferno* and in a considerable portion of the *Visio*.

31. A. H. Gilbert, *Dante's Conception of Justice,* cit., p. 108.

In the former the allegorical truth is conveyed through the vision of the penal conditions of the condemned souls, unendingly undergoing the severe punishment inflicted by God's inexorable justice and worked out by means of a strict law of commutative retaliation. This St. Thomas Aquinas called *contrapassum* and the poet uses it in order to reveal also the ugliness of sin itself as well as its personal and social consequences.

Besides, the whole topography of Hell, palpable and concrete as an earthly landscape, with its broken ledges, chasms, pits, swamps and rivers—all converging on the icy bottom occupied by the author of all malice—enriches the allegorical significance of the journey.[32] The downward, ever-narrowing path is a clear image of the progressive self-degrading movement by which sinful man instinctively precipitates himself towards the point of his own undoing, wilfully pursued. In Langland the message is conveyed more directly, I would suggest, through the crowded scenes of confused humanity, where with a quick tempo the allied forces of evil are shown, and set in motion, with the outwardly attractive power of cupidity placed in their midst in order to rally them, maliciously organizing their onslaught on mankind in order to overthrow truth, and corrupt justice. Together with this movement and action, from the Folk in the Field of the Prologue to the cavalcade to Westminster, the force of the argument is entrusted by the poet to the swift dialogues and debates between the spokesmen of Truth and the agents of Falsehood. It is by this that Langland succeeds in revealing with increasing effectiveness the basically dangerous nature of Lucre.

It is true that what makes Langland's vision of sinfulness distinctly unique and different from most medieval poems—particularly from the one we are trying to compare it with—is the almost complete absence of background, of a visible environment surrounding the action or echoing the discourse, which, as in

32. The material structure of Hell is so realistic that it is not wholly strange or surprising to find, in the century-long study of the *Divine Comedy*, attempts to measure the actual features and the extension of its fabric: "Galileo estimates, e.g., that Dante's Hell is about 4000 miles in depth and as many in breadth at its widest diameter". Quoted from *Dante, the Central Man of the World*, by J. T. Slattery, New York 1920, p. 128.

Dante, creates a fitting atmosphere, allegorically significant in itself and enhancing the moral drama of human perversion.[33] I say *"almost* complete absence"*, because a landscape is there even though barely hinted at, especially at the outset, and perhaps sufficient for the attentive reader to remember. But the lack of a realistic, consistent scenery, however desirable from the point of view of artistic completeness, is compensated for by the dynamic activity of a great number of characters and their lively repartee. Moreover, the various personifications of wickedness with their self-revealing names, their words and deeds, together with the throng of corrupt officials, really create around themselves a hellish atmosphere. No one can help sensing this when looking at or listening to Fauel, Gyle, Symonie and Cyuile, Lyere and Wronge, together with

> ... Piers the pardonere of Paulynes doctrine,
> Bette the bedel of Bokyngham-shire,
> Rainalde the reue of Rotland sokene,
> Munde the mellere and many moo other.
>
> (B, II, 108-10)
> [... Piers the pardoner of the Pauline Order,
> Barth the beadle of Buckinghamshire,
> Reynold the reeve of the district of Rutland,
> Mund the miller and very many others.]

All of them—dancing around Meed and Fals—are as overtly ugly as many of the *Inferno's* devils or as sordidly deceitful as many sinners of Dante's *Malebolge*, and smell as foul.[34] The farcical

---

33. As observed by Rosemary Woolf in an article on "Some Non-Medieval Qualities of *Piers Plowman*" in *Essays in Criticism*, XII, April 1962, p. 117. I do not agree that this fact "gives an impression of vagueness and greyness to the poem", as far at least as the *Visio* is concerned. Appropriately, however, Miss Woolf adds immediately after, that "the dominant tone ... of *Piers Plowman* is set by the verbs, which constantly suggest abrupt and vigorous action—action such as leaping, jumping or rushing—in a way that could not be sensibly visualized, and which bear no relation to the static scenes of art".

34. Professor Kane in this respect writes very much to the point: "he (Langland) uses this effect of ugliness to drive home the lesson of the

parody of Meed's marriage settlement with Fals, sealed with a mock-charter, contains, in a thickly condensed array, most of the sins and sinful dispositions which Dante scrutinizes in a more individualized and orderly fashion in the lower part of his under-world. And if, again, to that we add the scene of the rout to London—"one of the most fantastic *danses macabres* in litera-ture", as it has been called[35]—followed by the highly revealing retreat of Fraud, Guile and Liar into the appropriate channels of hidden traffickings (this episode, in tone, compares fittingly with the comic grotesqueness of the "trickish" world of grafters and barrators in *Inf.* XXI-XXII), we get, I think, a rather extensive picture of Langland's powerful visualization of evil. This is, to a considerable extent, his "vivido inferno quotidiano" as an Italian critic has defined it,[36] which corresponds in many aspects to that of Dante.

Perhaps one should mention in this connection also the Seven Deadly Sins, which will reiterate in a more distinctive way the theme of man's wilful transgression (Passus V), and would there-fore offer interesting analogies with some "figures" of the *Inferno.* Since, however, they are portrayed within the context of a scene of general repentance, it seems more opportune to place them, in structural terms, in relation to the *Purgatorio.* Nevertheless, as vivid examples of wrong humanized, enlarging and completing at the same time Langland's exposition of evil-doing, they must be included in the framework of analysis of sin, whose resemblance in the two poems we are trying to establish. I propose, however, to work out this comparison in literary terms (a more fruitful approach, I hope), later on. Here, for the moment, in order to

---

miserable condition of unregenerate man. The names of his allegorical characters stink of evil ... they are no less effectively unsavoury than the flesh and blood creatures with which he peoples his sordid underworld, Piers the Pardoner, Rainald the Reue ... a pack of some fifty in all who skulk about his poem adding the weight of their offences to the mass of evil under which he wishes us to see the world bowed" (op. cit., p. 231).

35. C. Brooke-Rose, "Ezra Pound: Piers Plowman in the Modern Waste Land" in *A Review of Engl. Literature*, II, April 1961, p. 77.

36. G. Baldini, *Storia della Letteratura Inglese,* Torino 1958, p. 140.

conclude the examination of the *Visio's* structural contents in relation to the first canticle of the *Commedia,* I wish to point out another important element of similarity between the two.

The clearly avowed purpose of the *Inferno*—indeed, its *raison d'etre*—is, as we saw, the unequivocal implementation of divine Law, the affirmation of an unflinching, superior Justice falling inexorably on the exposed folly of wicked creatures. Langland's sense of divine justice is as deeply felt as Dante's, and stated throughout with equally strong conviction, so as to form one of the leading motifs in the structure of the *Visio*. Obviously it is not as fully and as thoroughly displayed, but it is averred as demandingly and uncompromisingly, and with a similar measure of emphasis. There is in the *Visio* a considerable number of statements about the foreboding of everlasting doom waiting on the evil-doer, which recall the many encountered in the *Inferno*. Holy Church's words, e.g., on the Castle of Care:

> ... who-so cometh thereinne
> May banne that he borne was to body or to soule.
> (B, I, 61-2)
> [... whoso comes therein
> May curse that he was born in body or in soul.]

remind us of the first curse—the first choral blasphemy—uttered by the damned at the entrance of *Inferno:*

> Bestemmiavano Iddio e i lor parenti,
>   l'umana spezie e 'l luogo e 'l tempo e 'l seme
>   di lor semenza e di lor nascimenti.
> (*Inf.,* III, 103-5)
> [They blasphemed God and their parents, the humankind, the place, the time, and the seed of their begetting and of their birth.]

Similarly, her account of Hell's origin echoes Virgil's description of the same phenomenon in *Inf.,* XXXIV, 121:26, and is, in its Miltonic grandeur, more elaborate and circumstantial:

Ponam pedem in aquilone, et similis ero altissimo.
And alle that hoped it mighte be so none heuene mighte hem
    holde,
But fellen out in fendes likness nyne dayes togideres,
Til god of his goodnesse gan stable and stynte,
And garte the heuene to stekye and stonden in quiete.
Whan thise wikked went out wonderwise thei fellen,
Somme in eyre, somme in erthe and somme in helle depe;
Ac lucifer lowest lith of hem alle;
For pryde that he pult out his peyne hath none ende;
And alle that worche with wronge wenden hij shulle
After her deth day and dwelle with that shrewe.

                                        (B, I, 118-27)

[*I will sit in the region of the North, and will be like to the
    Most High.*
And all those who hoped that it might be so, heaven could
    hold no longer;
For they fell in the form of fiends for nine days together,
Until God in his mercy steadied and stopped their motion,
And caused the heavens to be closed and be again at peace.
When these wicked ones fell out in a strange way they fell
Some in the air, some on earth and some deep into hell;
But Lucifer lies lowest of them all;
Because of the pride that he put on his pain has no end;
And all those who act wrongly shall go
After the day of their death and dwell with that wretch.]

In a set of almost similar lines on the fatality of the chastisement
(Passus II, 99-106), the poet later stresses, by the double-edged
legalism of the rich promises contained in the marriage "feoffment", the tragic mockery of sin destined to self-defeat and
condemnation. Often the quotations from the Bible or the Fathers,
abundantly sown in the text by Langland, appear to be inserted
at random and are rather cumbersome. But sometimes, as in this
instance, they confer a particular effectiveness on the point he
wants to make. Thus, from "Ignis deuorabit tabernacula eorum
qui libenter accipiunt munera" (B, III, 95),[37] to "Nullum malum

... impunitum" (IV, 143) which we noted already as Reason's conclusion to his peroration to the king against Meed,[38]and many more of the same tenor, until we reach the most emphatic and solemn assertion of a Law which will stand and punish any attempt at flouting or frustrating it, and will call everyone to a final rendering of account:

Et qui bona egerunt, ibunt in vitam eternam;
Qui vero mala, in ignem eternum.

(B, VII, 111-12)
[*And they that have done good shall go into life everlasting:
And they that have done evil into everlasting fire.*]

This last clause of the Athanasian Creed constitutes the crowning point of the entire *Visio,* underlining the ineluctable severity of God's justice, under whose unshakable judgement Langland, like Dante, wants us to see all human life.[39] At this point most of the expositors and critics of *Piers Plowman* usually plunge headlong into digressive discussions in the attempt—necessary and valuable as it may be—to explain the meaning (a rather puzzling one, it must be admitted) of the pardon scene and the argument between Piers and the priest.[40] In so doing, however, they make us forget or overlook the stark simplicity of this dramatic statement and the centrality of its positioning. Such an univocal affirmation of the absolute law of God goes—I would suggest—straight back to the eternal realities implied in the two symbols of the Tower and the Dungeon in the Prologue. It encloses within an inescapable circle, as it were, the vision of universal blameworthiness which occupies the greater portion of the first part of *Piers Plowman* and thus runs parallel to the main theme of Dante's *Inferno.*

37. Given by the author as from the *Books of Solomon,* but being actually from *Job XV,* 34. Cf. Goodridge, op. cit., p. 323.

38. Above p. 56.

39. This epigrammatic distich seems to echo Dante's own definition of the meaning of the whole *Commedia*: "Si vero accipiatur opus allegorice, subiectum est homo, prout merendo et demerendo per arbitrii libertatem iustitiae praemiandi et puniendi obnoxius est" (quoted above, p. 29).

40. B. VII. 106-142

CHAPTER 3

THE THEME OF REPENTANCE

At the end of the foregoing chapter particular stress was laid on the second half of Truth's Pardon—those who do evil shall go into everlasting fire—in order to emphasize as completely as possible the degree of thematic correspondence of a relevant portion of the *Visio* with the *Inferno*. But we must also underline the positive element contained in that eschatological formula—the first half of which the poet manifestly intends us to keep in equal focus. On it, in fact, converges the dramatization of the other main theme of the *Visio*—the summons to general reform which the Folk in the Field willingly undertake, though their enthusiasm proves to be short-lived. The Pardon—I would prefer to define it rather as God's message—conveys also the promise of reward for the good, and follows the scenes of the Folk's repentance, their cheerful readiness to make amends and to set out again on the way to Truth. After the Confessions of the Seven Sins the poet offers to us a moving picture of incipient general conversion, enhanced by a splendid prayer for forgiveness which is also a cry of hope for sinful mankind :

And thanne had Repentance reuthe and redde hem alle to knele

. . . .

"Now god", quod he, "that of thi goodnesse gonne the worlde make,

And of naughte madest aughte and man moste liche to thiselue,

And sithen suffredest for to synne a sikeness to vs alle,

. . . .

And madest thi-self with thi sone and vs synful yliche,
. . . .
And sith with thi self sone in owre sute deydest
. . . .
And al that Marke hath ymade Mathew, Iohan, and Lucas,
Of thyne doughtiest dedes were don in owre armes;
Verbum caro factum est, et habitauit in nobis.
And bi so moche, me semeth the sikerere we mowe
Bydde and biseche if it be thi wille,
That art owre fader and owre brother be merciable to vs."
                          (B, V, 485; 488-90; 494; 495; 507-11)
[Then Repentance had pity and bade them all kneel:
. . . .

"Now God," he said, "that of your goodness made the world,
And from nought made all and man most like to yourself,
And after allowed him to sin, bringing sickness upon us all,
. . . .
And made yourself in the person of your son like us sinful
    men,
. . . .
And then with the same your son died in our flesh
. . . .
And as Mark has written, Matthew, John and Luke
All of your mightiest deeds were done in our human nature,
The Word was made flesh and dwelt among us,
And accordingly, it seems to me that we may more confidently
Pray and beseech you, if it be your will,
Who are our Father and our Brother, that you be merciful to
    us."]

The prayer evokes a resonant echo from the multitude, and

A thousand of men tho thrungen togyderes;
Criede vpward to Cryst and to his clene moder
To haue grace to go with hem Treuthe to seke.

                                    (ibid., 517-19)

[A thousand men then came thronging together,
And cried upward to Christ and to his pure Mother
To have the grace to go with them in search for Truth.]

But, bereft of guides, they "blunder on like beasts, over humps and hills" (line 521). It is a Plowman, the symbol of all righteous and honest behaviour, the incarnation of the human soul *natural-iter christiana,* who appears on the scene in order to show them the way. By observing the Ten Commandments and by fulfilling their worldly duties (or better, their feudal duties, according to the poet's social outlook)—each acknowledging the demands of his *status,* together with reliance on divine grace and mercy, men can reach Truth and salvation. From Piers the Plowman's demand for help to plough his half-acre and the agreement to do so on the part of some willing members of the Folk, we can derive the suggestion of a close connection between material and spiritual work—an important aspect of *Piers Plowman,* and one which is peculiar to the poem.[1] The "spiritualization" of work as a necessary and valid element of any true moral progress is a prominent motif of the second part of the *Visio,* and in this Langland, when compared with Dante, stands out as a completely original poet in his moral probings.[2] In the *Commedia* we have scarcely any overt mention of humble social or material problems, nor any outstanding reference to or awareness of the "sociological" in the modern sense, such

1. G. R. Owst, *Preaching in Medieval England,* Cambridge 1926, drew attention to this point when dealing with the poem. Emphasizing Langland's "unqualified praise of the labouring poor" (p. 296), Dr. Owst showed the connection of the motif with the sermon literature of the time. As a significant example of this he refers to the "canonization of hard work" in Nicole Bozon's *Contes Moralizés* (p. 301). See also *Literature and Pulpit in Medieval England,* Cambridge 1933, where Dr. Owst considers this subject more extensively (pp. 565-74).
2. This human dimension of *Piers Plowman* makes its author still more strikingly different from the contemporary English poets, who like Chaucer or the poet of *Sir Gawain* or *Pearl* seem to be unaware of the events of 1381 such as the Peasants' Revolt, or of the Black Death. An exception in this respect could be admitted in the case of *Wynnere and Wastoure* and *The Parlement of the Three Ages.*

as pervades the English poem and gives it its unique flavour.[3] The needs of the body, the necessities of temporal life and their satisfaction as a preliminary stage in the development of the harmoniously ordered life of a human being—with which the problem of poverty and the right use of riches are connected—are as prominent and searchingly dealt with in *Piers Plowman* as they are almost absent in the *Divine Comedy*.[4] Piers's half-successful effort to set the world to work reflects the poet's intense interest in the real social problems of his time—famine, idleness, social justice—and is placed within the general movement of moral and spiritual regeneration. It represents the constructive side of the poem, a positive counterpart to the previous destructive vision of sin and corruption. The structural pattern of the *Visio*, in fact, consists of a series of negative moments which alternate with positive statements, the continuous affirmation of ideal truths against the grim reality of actual life. Thus, the Prologue's vision of wayward humanity is followed by Holy Church's teachings, and the disruptive workings of Cupidity (Lady Meed) are balanced by the intervention of Reason and Conscience, while a further investigation of sin and frailty leads to another detailed mapping of the way to Truth. Obviously, therefore, while the negative aspects of the *Visio* can be said to parallel, partly at least, the more thorough investigation of *Inferno* (as we have tried to show), the positive features, however improperly isolated from the whole context, must be related to the allegory of moral and spiritual progress visualized in Dante's *Purgatorio*. But, although the general movement of Passus V, VI and VII points clearly to a collective effort to turn away from sin and to start anew on the path of amendment with a view to achieving a more positive good, the pilgrimage proposed by Piers to his fellow-creatures is not actually carried out. The reason

3. Cf. Holy Church's speech on food, drink and clothing (I, 17-42; 54-7) and the episode of Hunger in VI, 107ff.

4. Perhaps it would be more correct to say that such problems and their solutions are treated by Dante in a more theoretical fashion or that they are implicit in the overall perspective of his moral and religious thought. For direct references to the dispensation of worldly goods cf. Virgil's speech on Fortune, *Inf.*, VII, 67-96. See also the question of the various social callings, *Par.* VIII, 139-48.

is, Fr. Dunning suggests, "because the reform of society is not possible on a corporate basis: it is achieved when each individual reforms himself".[5] This was indicated already by Piers himself in the final clause of his last will, made before setting his hand to the plough to provide for the community:

And with the residue and the remenaunte bi the rode of Lukes!
I wil worschip ther-with Treuthe bi my lyue,
And ben his pilgryme atte plow for pore mennes sake.
(B, VI, 102-4)

[And with all that is left to me, I swear by the Cross of Lucca,
I will worship Truth therewith while I live,
And be his pilgrim at the plough for poor men's sake.]

Honest labour can go hand in hand with a simple and wholesome faith. Nevertheless a truly spiritual life requires more than that. It implies a more active "service" of Truth. And Piers later becomes aware of this when, perceiving the wide meaning of *"qui bona egerunt"*, he argues with a learned priest who has questioned the "legal" validity of the Pardon, and

... for pure tene pulled it atweyne,
And seyde, *"si ambulavero in medio umbre mortis,*
        non timebo mala; quoniam tu mecum es.
I shal cessen of my sowyng," quod Pieres, "and swynk nought so harde,
Ne about my bely-ioye so bisi be namore!
Of preyers and of penaunce my plow shal ben herafter,
And wepen whan I shulde slepe though whete-bred me faille."
(B, VII, 116-20)

[... in sheer rage tore it in two
And said: *"Though I walk through the valley of the shadow of death, I will fear no evil: for thou art with me."*
"I shall cease from my sowing," said Piers, "and toil not so hard,

---

5. "The Structure of the B Text", *RES*, vii, p. 232.

> Nor be so busy any more about my belly-joy!
> Of prayer and of penance my plough shall be hereafter,
> And I will weep when I should sleep though I lack wheaten
>   bread."]

Yet, the solemn declaration of the good Plowman, the servant of
Truth, to lead from now on a more fervent life of prayer and
penance, remains, with all his eager acceptance of God's message,
an affirmation in principle of the existence of a life higher than
that of simple observance of the Commandments. The pardon
scene, concluding the first important series of revelatory dreams,
serves not only to reaffirm dramatically God's immutable law,
but, denying the value of money-purchased bulls and of merely
external acts of religion,[6] points to the realization of a more
genuine spiritual life whose starting point is the doctrine of *Ne
solliciti sitis* (line 126). As Fr. Dunning says: "The Pardon initiates
a new kind of pilgrimage: the progress of the soul in the spiritual
life".[7] But whilst Piers, responding unreservedly to the new call,
embarks readily on its fulfilment, the Dreamer becomes only
vaguely aware of its importance, and starts musing on the meaning
of *Doing Well*:

> And al this maketh me on this meteles to thynke;
> And how the prest preued no pardoun to Dowel,
> And demed that Dowel indulgences passed,
> Biennales and triennales and bisschopes lettres,

6. I accept in this regard the conclusions of R. W. Frank Jr. who has
explained, convincingly I think, the meaning of the pardon scene: "Just as
Piers' Testament is not really a will but a device for communicating an
ethical message by means of the contrast between the conventional form
and its novel content, so too the pardon is not really an orthodox pardon
but a device for stating an ethical principle dramatically . . . In accepting its
message, Piers is rejecting bulls with seals." The act of tearing a worthless
piece of paper, continues Frank, "was intended as a sign that Piers had
rejected indulgences and accepted the command to do well. Unfortunately,
it was a very confusing sign" (*Piers Plowman and the Scheme of Salvation*,
Yale Univ. Press 1957, p. 28; cf. also Dunning, *The A Text*, pp. 145-52).
   7. "The Structure of the B Text", *RES*, vii, p. 232.

And how Dowel at the day of dome is dignelich vnderfongen,
And passeth al the pardoun of seynt Petres cherche.

(B, VII, 167-72)

[And all this makes me ponder on this dream;
And how the priest proved that no pardon could compare with
    Do-well,
And deemed that Do-well was superior to indulgences,
Biennals, triennals, and Bishops' letters,
And how Do-well at Doomsday will be honourably received
And surpass all the pardons of St. Peter's Church.]

We must not forget that the Dreamer, as the recipient of the many
visions which constitute the structural divisions of the poem, is
the principal character for whose benefit these visions take place.
He must be taken therefore as the logical protagonist of the
narrative. The progressive enlightenment of Will the Dreamer, as
he travels along the paths of self-knowledge, moral discipline and
intellectual speculation, takes place in the *Vita de Dowel, Dobet,
et Dobest*. It is mainly with the *Purgatorio*—where Dante the
Pilgrim goes through a similar process—that we can compare the
second part of *Piers Plowman*. I say *mainly*, because the *Vita*
presents certain features and contains problems which are also
present in the *Paradiso*.

It goes without saying that the narrative of the middle *cantica*
of the *Commedia* has very little in common with the second section
of *Piers Plowman*. The same can be said as regards the landscape.
In the *Purgatorio* it forms not only the ideal or emotional background of the action but the essential support for the structural
organization of the whole allegory. In comparison, only a few of
the dreams occurring in *Dowel, Dobet* and *Dobest* are visualized
within a framework of significant pictorial features which sharpen
the contours of an episode and enhance the dramatization of an
idea. It is therefore chiefly by relating the general movement of
Purgatorio and the main stages of the upward journey to the
"story" of the Dreamer in the *Vita*, and by assessing their individual as well as universal applications, that we can detect elements
of analogous development. In order to do that I propose to sum-

marize in the following pages, as concisely as possible, the literal
contents first of *Purgatorio* then of *Dowel, Dobet* and *Dobest*,
integrating our analysis with the appropriate allegorical interpretation of each.[8] As a result we shall be in a position to establish,
subsequently, the existence of important "areas of agreement"
between the two.

From the gloomy depths of Hell Dante and Virgil have landed
on the shores of the ocean which covers the southern hemisphere.
From its centre rises, lofty and solemn, the Mountain of Purgatory
reaching up to search the very sky. The "sweet hue of oriental
sapphire", the shining of the beauteous planet Venus "che d'amar
conforta" together with four glimmering stars, and the sun rising
in the peaceful dawn of Easter Sunday, are the encouraging
features of the new atmosphere of renewal. They will accompany
in varied shapes and degrees the "pilgrim's progress". These
aspects of nature do make an enchanting picture of idyllic peace
and rapture. At the same time, they are charged with deep symbolism, and from their contemplation we are plunged into a
dramatic scene which is important to the whole "story" of *Purgatorio*. The rays of the four stars, symbolic of the Cardinal Virtues
—absent from our world at present, says the poet—are reflected
on the forehead of Cato, the warden of this second realm,

> dove l'umano spirito si purga
> e di salire al ciel diventa degno.
>
> *(Purg.,* I, 5-6)
>
> [where the human spirit is purged and becomes fit to ascend
> to Heaven.]

With a stern, almost violent, apostrophe, this venerable and aus-
tere old man challenges the Pilgrim and his guide as if they were
fugitives from Hell trying to break the immutable laws of the other
world. Virgil pleads with him for his own disciple, eloquently

8. I am perfectly aware that such a method might be questioned as being
likely to result in part in a lengthy and not so necessary paraphrase of the
narratives. But I feel this is the only way to validate, critically, the comparative approach I have adopted in the present study.

trying to win Cato's favour by recalling the great love he had for the chaste Marcia, for whose sake he should let them go and visit his "sette regni". But no rhetoric of earthly bonds of affections can move Cato. It is only when he is told that the Pilgrims are making the journey by divine decree and with the assistance of a heavenly lady, that he bids Virgil to cleanse Dante with dew and gird him with a rush from a meadow on the sea-shore. "Then, concludes Cato, let not your return be by this way. The sun, which is now rising will show you the way to take the Mount by an easier ascent" (I, 106-8). The transparent symbolism of this initial scene brings into focus the condition of the human soul in a dramatic moment of its experience. Having disentangled itself at last from the bonds of sin, it gains moral freedom and can now set out on the way of penance and redemption. At the beginning the spirit abandons itself, with an immediate sense of relief, to the new state, but is put almost abruptly in front of the great responsibility which such new conditions involve. The Suicide of Utica (traditionally considered as the highest example of pagan morality on account of his life's sacrifice for the sake of Roman liberty) is here assumed as the fitting "figure" of the absolute selflessness and complete sense of duty,[9] necessary for the attainment of spiritual freedom. But if the natural virtues are the true foundation of this moral imperative, they will be validated only by being wholly reorientated towards and taken up into Christian spirituality where Divine Grace can strengthen and perfect them. Fortified by these demanding yet so encouraging premises—they will set the tone of the whole *cantica* through being continually reaffirmed and developed—Dante the Pilgrim, always assisted by his Guide, can start now on his way up. The going will, on the whole, be steady, uninterrupted; there will be delays and setbacks, though, because the path of virtue is strewn with hardships and the warp of sin together with worldly inclinations can still make the will waver. At the very beginning of the journey, in fact, while the hymn of

---

9. In his previous works Dante had already exalted Cato as the most heroic champion of moral freedom, and, as such, worthy of resembling God Himself. Cf. *Conv.* IV, v, 16; xxviii, 15; xxviii, 19; *Monarchia*, II, v, 15.

deliverance *In exitu Israel de Egypto,* chanted by a group of souls just ferried by an angel to the island, fittingly points to the new direction, we have the first of such moments of lagging. Among these souls Dante recognizes his friend Casella the musician. While all the shades and the two poets wander around uncertain of the way, the old musician, at Dante's request, intones one of the latter's own odes, and everybody listens enraptured.[10] The enchantment is broken by Cato, who severely chides them for lingering, in wasteful distraction from the more important business. Human friendship, poetry and music, arts and literature, especially philosophical speculation, are not a sin in the sight of God, but can clearly become such if they cause a distracting delay in the process of redemption.[11] In this moment of uncertainty and forgetfulness the firm voice of Conscience rises to reprimand and reorientate will (Dante) and reason (Virgil).

The two wayfarers now reach the foot of the Mountain which rises steep and almost inaccessible:

> quivi trovammo la roccia sì erta,
> che 'ndarno vi sarien le gambe pronte.
>
> (*Purg.,* III, 47-8)
>
> [there we found the cliff so steep
> that the nimblest legs would have been useless on it.]

It seems that the human forces are not adequate to the task and Virgil, who does not know the way up, has to admit the limitation of natural reason in grasping the things of a supernatural order (ibid., lines 31-45). In the rocky perimeter there is a narrow crevice to which they are directed by the souls of the excommunicated who, although saved, must here wait thirty times as long as

10. *"Amor che nella mente mi ragiona",* one of the poems written by Dante in praise of the *Donna Gentile,* personification of Philosophy, and commented on by him in *Conv.* III, 12.

11. This episode indicates that Dante here is recanting, above all, his former excessive enthusiasms for Aristotelian philosophy and eager intellectual speculation which, he now seems to recognize, might be dangerous for the orthodoxy of religious truth.

the ban of the Church lasted. And so Virgil continues to assist and encourage in the arduous climb:

> Ed elli a me: "Nessun tuo passo caggia:
> pur su al monte dietro a me acquista,
> fin che n'appaia alcuna scorta saggia".

> (*Purg.*, IV, 37-9)

> [And he said to me: "Do not fall back a step;
> still make thy way up the mountain behind me
> till some wise guide appear for us."]

Passing through a steep and rugged crack, almost a fissure cut in the rock, proves too much for the weary Pilgrim, and when at last they reach an open ledge, Virgil describes the nature of the Mount: climbing it requires hardest labour at first, only to become easier and easier in the process of ascending:

> "Questa montagna è tale,
> che sempre al cominciar di sotto è grave;
> e quant'uom più va su, e men fa male.
> Però, quand'ella ti parrà soave
> tanto, che su andar ti fia leggiero
> com'a seconda giù andar per nave,
> allor sarai al fin d'esto sentiero:
> quivi di riposar l'affanno aspetta.
> Più non rispondo, e questo so per vero."

> (*Purg.*, IV, 88-96)

> ["This mountain is such that
> it is always hard at the start below and the
> higher one goes it is less toilsome.
> Therefore when it will seem to thee so pleasant
> that going up will be so easy for thee
> as going downstream in a boat, then thou
> shalt be at the end of this path: There look
> to rest thy weariness. I have no more to answer,
> and this I know for truth."]

The acquisition of virtue is slow and painful. In the end, however, there is a promise of true freedom and spiritual wholeness.
For the moment, on the other hand, further instances of negligence
and bewilderment must be experienced, even if only by the closeness of some encounter, or by the observation of the souls' condition. After resting on the ledge, Dante proceeds on his way and
on a slope comes across the Indolent. He stops awhile in order to
talk to Belacqua, an old friend from Florence, crouched down in
a posture of extreme laziness—a living statue of sluggishness.
Further up the travellers meet the Unshriven, those who died of
violence after deferring their repentance to the last hour, and then
they arrive at the Valley of the Preoccupied, Kings and Princes
who, owing to their temporal concerns and cares of state, also put
off their conversion to the last moment.[12] Sordello, a fellow-
Mantuan of Virgil's, leads the pilgrims and points to the various
spirits. These, true to their former characteristic fault, speak of
their families, praise the worth of good monarchs on earth, and
condemn the degeneracy of others. Night is falling and according
to the law of the Mountain the pilgrims cannot proceed after
sunset. As Sordello explains, without the light of the sun, that is
without the illumination of God's grace, no real progress in the
good life is possible. And here, at the end of the first day spent by
Dante in Purgatory, during this temporary darkness of the night
as well as of the soul, occurs the "figuration" of an ever-recurring
event in the life of man. It is the nightly assault of the Serpent:
creeping towards the dismayed souls, he approaches to remind
them of their former weakness. The hymn of compline—*Te lucis
ante terminum*—rises from the spirits and the serpent is chased
away by two angels who descend "from Mary's bosom" to defend

12. In the commentary to her translation of *Purgatorio* (Penguin Books,
London 1955, p. 122), Dorothy L. Sayers aptly comments on this point:
"Dante in his vision is shown only the most striking and illustrious representatives in each category; but we need not doubt that he would place in
this class not only kings and statesmen, but also humbler examples of the
Preoccupied, such as anxious parents, over-burdened housewives and bread-
winners, social workers, busy organizers, and others who are so 'rushed off
their feet' that they forget to say their prayers". Miss Sayers' remarks sound
really Langlandian: one is reminded of the character Haukyn, Activa Vita
in *Dowel*, Passus XIII.

them from the ancient adversary. Rather than for the penitent
souls gathered here in fear and expectation, this scene of temptation
is perhaps more significantly enacted for the living pilgrim, who
learns to have trust in divine help in these moments of "the
involuntary aberrations of the unconscious".[13] To comfort him,
in fact, and give assurance to his troubled mind, three bright stars
have replaced the four seen at daybreak:

> Gli occhi miei ghiotti andavan pur al cielo,
> E 'l duca mio: "Figliuol, che là su guarde?"
> E io a lui: "A quelle tre facelle
> di che 'l polo di qua tutto quanto arde."
>
> (*Purg.*, VIII, 85; 88-90)
>
> [My greedy eyes kept going to the sky,
> And my Leader asked me: "Son what art thou gazing
> at up there?" And I answered him: "At those three
> torches with which the pole here is aflame."]

By their glimmering against the dark sky these "torches" show
forth the light of the Theological Virtues. Gradually we are leaving
behind the world of Ante-Purgatory, abode of the Late Repentant
and image of a wayward humanity, still wandering in a state of
spiritual instability, and we are approaching the stage of a more
determined and positive renewal. This will take place within the
active presence of Grace and under the aegis of the Church's
authority. Dante sleeps, and near dawn dreams of being carried
by a golden-feathered eagle into the sphere of fire. But his dream,
as often in the *Commedia*, is prophetic, a presage of immediately
subsequent happenings. On awakening he learns from Virgil that
he has actually been carried by St. Lucy to the gate of Purgatory
proper. God's Grace and Justice (Lucy and the eagle) have inter-
vened jointly to assist the soul, landing it upon the sacramental
ground of active penitence. Helped by his Guide, Dante mounts
the three steps of Confession, Contrition and Satisfaction, humbles
himself in front of the Angel-keeper who is armed with St. Peter's
keys—the power invested in the Priesthood to bind or unloose.

---

13. D. L. Sayers, op. cit., p. 130.

After branding Dante's forehead with seven Ps—the sign of the Capital Sins, the Porter lets him through the adamantine portal. Meantime the strains of *Te Deum laudamus* welcome the new penitent. Now, within the central division of this uniquely Christian place of expiation, the eradication of the roots of sin will take place by the expunging of its remnants. It is by crossing the seven terraces of pride, envy, anger, sloth, avarice and prodigality, gluttony and lust, that Dante is shown the essence of sin and frees himself from its tendencies by sharing, directly or indirectly, in the temporal punishment of the penitent souls, and by heeding the examples illustrating each sin or the opposite virtue. The Bible, sacred and profane history, mythology supply in turn the material for these vivid tableaux which Divine Art displays in order to admonish and instruct. When, at each round, the lesson has been learnt—not just from the eloquence of these pictures, but more, and perhaps mainly, through the encounters with various penitent spirits (it is from the personal stories of some of them that we get a deep insight into the way each vice originates and operates in the human psyche), the Ps are erased from Dante's brow, and he can reach the earthly Paradise. Cleansed and purified, man becomes as innocent as his spirit was when it first issued from its Maker's hands. Eden is regained.

Thus expounded the Pilgrim's journey and the progress of the soul appear to have followed an expeditious course. And so, in fact, it is—straightforward and with no break of continuity. However, true to his purpose of fully representing the conflict inherent in the Christian moral life with its failures and triumphs, the poet has interposed in the story two more dreams which are indicative of this twofold reality. The first occurs when, having purged the sinful inclinations of pride, envy, wrath and sloth—the aberrations typical of the mind, Dante, before the dawn of the second day spent in Purgatory, sees in a revelatory dream the Siren of incontinence—a vision foreshadowing the vices of covetousness, gluttony and lust that are expiated in the next three terraces. But the dream is more than an appropriate element of structure; it stands out as a vivid insight into the auto-suggestion of the mind beguiled by the alluring power of sensual passion. It appears first as a "femina balba", "a stuttering female", ugly and repulsive, exactly as vice is in reality. But the dreaming Pilgrim gazes insistently upon her,

> ... e come 'l sol conforta
> le fredde membra che la notte aggrava,
> così lo sguardo mio le facea scorta
> la lingua, e poscia tutta la drizzava
> in poco d'ora, e lo smarrito volto,
> com'amor vuol, così le colorava.
>
> (Purg., XIX, 10-14)
>
> [... and as the sun revives
> cold limbs benumbed by the night, so my look
> gave her a ready tongue and then in a little
> time made her quite erect and coloured her
> wan features as love desires.]

And from the transformed Siren's mouth flows the sweet song promising the gratification of all desires:

> "Io son", cantava, "io son dolce serena,
>   che i marinari in mezzo mar dismago;
>   tanto son di piacere a sentir piena!
> Io volsi Ulisse del suo cammin vago
>   al canto mio; e qual meco si aùsa,
>   rado sen parte; sì tutto l'appago!"
>
> (ibid., 19-24)
>
> ["I am," she sang, "I am the sweet siren
> who beguiles the sailors in mid-sea,
> so great delight it is to hear me.
> I turned Ulysses, eager on his way, to my song,
> and he who dwells with me rarely departs,
> so wholly I content him."]

The enchantment is broken by the intervention of Virgil, who prompted by a mysterious Lady, uncovers the enchantress's womb, whose foul stench awakens the sleeper. It is time again to cast away the temptations of worldly pleasures, and to turn the eyes to the

> ... logoro che gira
> lo rege eterno con le rote magne.
>
> (ibid., 62-3)
>
> [to the lure which the Eternal King
> spins with the great wheel.]

The other dream—the last of the three experienced in Purgatory
—is a complement of the previous one and, at the same time, a
foreboding of the state of incipient perfection which the Pilgrim
is about to reach. On emerging from the fire of the last terrace in
which the sins of lust are cleansed, on the very threshold of the
Garden of Eden, Dante dreams of Leah and Rachel, the two
sisters of the Old Testament, traditional personifications of the
Active Life and the Contemplative:

> Ne l'ora, credo, che de l'oriente
>   prima raggió nel monte Citerea,
>   che di foco d'amor par sempre ardente,
> giovane e bella in sogno mi parea
>   donna vedere andar per una landa
>   cogliendo fiori; e cantando dicea:
> "Sappia qualunque il mio nome dimanda
>   ch'io mi son Lia, e vo movendo intorno
>   le mani a farmi una ghirlanda.
> Per piacermi a lo specchio, qui m'adorno;
>   ma mia suora Rachel mai non si smaga
>   dal suo miraglio, e siede tutto giorno.
> Ell'è de' suoi belli occhi veder vaga,
>   com'io de l'adornarmi con le mani;
>   lei lo veder, e me l'ovrare appaga."
>
> (*Purg.,* XXVII, 94-108)
>
> [In the hour, I think, when Cytherea, who seems
> always burning with the fire of love, first shone
> on the mountain from the east, I seemed to see
> in a dream a lady young and beautiful going
> through a meadow gathering flowers and singing:
> "Know, whoever asks my name, that I am Leah,

> and I go plying my fair hands here and there to
> make me a garland; to please me at the glass I here
> adorn myself, but my sister Rachel never leaves her
> mirror and sits all day. She is fain to see her own
> fair eyes as I to adorn me with my hands.
> She with seeing, and I with doing am satisfied."]

In a dozen lines the poet has encompassed a perfectly enchanting picture where music, colour, ethereal beauty combine harmoniously with a precise allegorical meaning. A reader of "pure" poetry will here pay attention to the pictorial element, to the rhythm of the verse or the grace of Leah's bearing. "Lia," notes an Italian critic e.g., "non dice che va 'cogliendo fiori', ma 'Vo movendo intorno/Le belle mani a farmi una ghirlanda', sottolineando il ritmo delle mani e la loro bellezza; e tutto il resto della sua parlata vagheggia amorosamente la sua figura a quella della sorella: sicché tutto si move ancora in un'aura di canto e d'incanto, *e il lettore amante della poesia non si sente frastorntao dall'allegoria.*"[14] ["Leah does not say she goes around 'picking flowers', but 'I go moving my fair hands around to make me a garland', underlying the rhythm of her hands and their beauty; all the rest of her speech focuses lovingly on her own figure and that of her sister: so that everything moves in an atmosphere of song and enchantment, and the reader who loves poetry does not feel distracted by allegory."] But I do not see why one cannot enjoy the poetry and appreciate at the same time the relevance of the symbol, without being necessarily "frastornato" (diverted) by the latter.[15] On the contrary, while being fascinated by the captivating image, we have to heed the poet's primary intention in writing these lines. The symbolism—it needs no subtle interpretation—is plainly meant to illustrate how to the soul that has conquered itself now opens the wide perspective of fruitful action and contemplation, the two complementary aspects of the perfect

14. A. Momigliano, op. cit., p. 472. Italics mine.
15. The same consideration applies to the vision of Matelda, (XXVIII, 1-51). Here, too, poetical "figure" and symbol are "totally" blended and cannot be arbitrarily split.

Christian life, which, incidentally, will be more concretely represented in the figures of Matelda and Beatrice in the radiant beauty
of the Earthly Paradise. Here, in the idyllic setting of a perfect
nature, where the recreated myth of the Golden Age enhances the
poignant feeling of happiness lost and refound, Dante, whose
nature and will have been restored to true freedom, is no longer
in need of human wisdom and of human science. Virgil has fulfilled his mission and, being no longer competent to guide him
higher, is about to leave his disciple's side:

> Come la scala tutta sotto noi
> > fu corsa e fummo in su 'l grado superno,
> > in me ficcò Virgilio li occhi suoi,
> e disse: "Il temporal foco e l'eterno
> > veduto hai, figlio; e se' venuto in parte
> > dov'io per me più oltre non discerno.
> Tratto t'ho qui con ingegno e con arte;
> > lo tuo piacere omai prendi per duce:
> > fuor se' de l'erte vie, fuor se' dell'arte.
> Vedi lo sol che in fronte ti riluce;
> > vedi l'erbetta, i fiori e li arbuscelli,
> > che qui la terra sol da sé produce.
> Mentre che vegnan lieti li occhi belli
> > che, lacrimando, a te venir mi fenno,
> > seder ti puoi e puoi andar tra elli.
> Non aspettar mio dir più né mio cenno:
> > libero, dritto e sano è tuo arbitrio,
> > e fallo fòra non fare a suo senno:
> per ch'io te sovra te corono e mitrio."

(Purg., XXVII, 124-42)

> [When all the stair was sped beneath us and we were
> on the topmost step Virgil fixed his eyes on me
> and said: "The temporal fire and the eternal thou
> hast seen, my son, and art come to a part where
> of myself I discern no further. I have brought thee
> here with understanding and with skill. Take henceforth

thy pleasure for guide. Thou hast come forth from
the steep and narrow ways. See the sun that
shines on thy brow; see the grass, the flowers and
trees which the ground here brings forth of itself
alone; till the fair eyes come rejoicing which
weeping made me come to thee thou mayest sit or
go among them. No longer expect word or sign
from me. Free, upright and whole is thy will and
it were a fault not to act on its bidding; therefore
over thyself I crown and mitre thee."]

The pilgrim is now ready to enter the living world of Faith where
his soul can come face to face with the presence of Christ, feel the
effect of His sacramental grace and be received into full communion with His Church.

Having reviewed thus summarily the second *Cantica* of the
Commedia through a simultaneous consideration of its literal and
allegorical levels, we have to ask ourselves: in what way and to
what extent can the second part of *Piers Plowman* be said to
correspond to the *Purgatorio*? We would look in vain for any
precise likenesses of content or external structure. But in the similarity of a general motif, of a movement along which the protagonist of the *Vita*[16] goes through the hardships of the Christian
life with the aim of attaining a spiritual certainty, there is a clear
parallel. The search for this *ubi consistam* eagerly pursued by an
erratic Dreamer who, eventually, is rewarded with the revelation
of a Truth, simple and whole at the same time, is the only possible
thread of narrative consistency offered to the reader, and, in our
case, the main element susceptible of providing some degree of
analogy when comparing the allegory of the *Vita* with that of the
Purgatorio.

The formal division of the middle Canticle of Dante's poem into

16. The word *Vita* does not, actually, figure in the manuscript headings
either of each section or of the titles of the Passus in B and C. It occurs
only at the end of Passus VIII of A. Cf. Skeat's edition, p. 251. I use it,
however, as a convenient, comprehensive term for this part of the poem as
is the general practice with *Piers Plowman* scholars.

three parts—Ante-Purgatory, Purgatory proper, and Earthly Paradise—each containing a clearly-marked phase in the pilgrimage of
the soul towards God, rendered the task of making a synopsis of
it a relatively easy one. Things are quite different with the second
part of Langland's work, for a corresponding organic arrangement
can hardly be found in the *Vita*. Even if we consider this section
of the English poem in itself and not in relation to any other
exemplar—not to say "archetype"—of medieval literature, the
structure of the *Vita* presents itself, on the surface at least, as
complex and rather unsystematic. The threefold division indicated
by the titles—*Dowel, Dobet,* and *Dobest* (each, according to the
manuscript headings, being the subject treated by the author
respectively in Passus VIII-XIV, XV-XVIII, and XIX-XX)—
does not seem to contain the organic progression that one would
expect from the comparative notions expressed by the three terms.
Yet progression there must be as it is clearly implied by the poet's
choice of these terms.

Only in relatively recent times have critics and exegetes of the
poem given a considerable amount of attention to this problem
with a view to explaining the meaning of the terms and thus
attempting to find a satisfactory interpretation of the *Vita*.[17]
Up to about ten years ago, two main interpretations, or sets of
interpretations, stood out and were widely accepted, with some
variations and modifications, by the majority of critics. The first,
advanced by Henry W. Wells, centred upon the suggestion that
Do-wel deals with and defines the Active Life, and is illustrated
in the *Dowel* section; Do-bet concerns the Contemplative Life and
is pictured in *Dobet;* Do-best treats of the Mixed or Prelatical
Life in the last section, *Dobest*.[18] The second was proposed by

17. Jusserand, one of the earlier critics of the poem, was content with
remarking that "Dowel, Dobet, and Dobest have two or three different
meanings". At the close of his study then, he selected one definition: *Disce,
Doce, Dilige* to define the triad (cf. op. cit., p. 155; 185).

18. "The Construction of Piers Plowman", *PMLA,* LXIV (1929), pp.
123-40. Following Wells's interpretation Nevill K. Coghill stresses further
the vocational nature of these three states, seeing Dowel, Dobet and Dobest
as ideals each characteristic of the laity, the clergy and the episcopacy. He
suggests, moreover, that they are best embodied in Piers respectively in the
Visio, in *Dobet* and *Dobest*: "The Character of Piers Plowman Considered

Professor H. Meroney who, in contrast with Wells's view, suggested that Dowel, Dobet, and Dobest, in accordance with the mystic tradition, are meant to portray the Purgative, Illuminative and Unitive Ways, as the three sequential stages of the soul's progress towards God.[19] Professor Donaldson accepts Meroney's solution while recognizing the importance of the Wells-Coghill theory and tries to reconcile them both in a more general and comprehensive concept, holding that the *Vita* deals contemporaneously with two different ideas. He writes:

> The *Vita* handles two basically different concepts at the same time and sometimes in the same terms. The chief difference between the concepts is that the first, as applied to the life of the individual, seems to develop in a sequence from out- wardness (the active life) to inwardness (the contemplative life) to inward-outwardness (the mixed life), while the second develops in a sequence of three stages of inwardness, all of which, of course, have also appropriate outward manifesta- tions and all of which are, incidentally, open to men of all vocations.[20]

In line with this trend of thought Fr. Dunning endeavours to show likewise how the two traditional concepts, "as distinguished by the medieval theologians and spiritual writers", are successfully blended and how they operate together in shaping the structure of the poem.[21]

Now, I do recognize that the interpretations advanced by these critics offer many valuable insights, and that their contributions go a long way in helping the non-specialist (like myself) to acquire a better understanding of the poem. Nevertheless, while I have—as everybody should have—the greatest respect for what I would call

from the B Text", *Medium Aevum,* II (1933), pp. 108-35. R. W. Chambers also agrees with these views, although his conclusions vary somewhat from those of Wells and Coghill. Cf. *Man's Unconquerable Mind,* op. cit., p. 102 ff.; 127 ff.
19. "The Life and Death of Longe Wille", *ELH,* XVII : 1950), p. 10 ff.
20. *Piers Plowman: the C Text and Its Poet,* p. 159.
21. "The Structure of the B Text of P.P.", *RES,* vii, pp. 225-37.

the "critical honesty" of the above-mentioned scholars, I must confess, with equal honesty, that the theories and the solutions proposed by them seem to me rather "over-ingenious" and somewhat inadequate for a satisfactory explanation of the structural unity of the poem. A lengthy and detailed discussion of the merits or demerits inherent in the "three lives" approach, if not altogether out of place here, would be somehow beyond the limits of our study and would take us far from its specific purpose. In the way of a general observation, however, I should like to qualify my objections to accepting unreservedly such views by noting, as regards the first set of correspondences, that the Active Life, the Contemplative Life and the Mixed Life are, indeed, prominent in the *Vita de Dowel, Dobet et Dobest*. They are, however, not "realized" but "discussed", investigated as progressive ideals of the good life *all together and at the same time* in the *Dowel* section. Here they are presented in an endless series of multiple definitions and counter-definitions through a kind of scholastic debate which will, in the end, reveal itself as rather sterile if not completely profitless. Then, in *Dobet,* these ideals of perfection are revealed in a dramatic fashion as being fulfilled through Christ's supreme example which goes beyond and transcends all theoretical distinctions, to be shown again as more often betrayed than implemented, in *Dobest*.[22] Seen in such a perspective, the presence of the first "triad" in the *Vita* and its use by the poet in relation to the abstract terms Dowel, Dobet and Dobest seem rather fluid; the correspondence between the "three lives" and the section titles is not systematic and cannot, therefore, be based on the correlation originally suggested by H. W. Wells.[23] If, on the other hand, we

22. Cf. J. J. Lawlor, op. cit., pp. 299-306. Prof. Lawlor's arguments against the validity of any group of "lives" or "ways" for explaining the structure of the *Vita,* are cogent and convincing. I am much indebted to him in this paragraph, although my conclusions are only in part based on his premises.

23. R. W. Frank also questions Wells' and Coghill's interpretations and suggests that "Dowel, Dobet and Dobest are not 'terms', each with a fixed meaning, but are rather divisions of the generic term 'Dowel'. It follows that there is no relation between the explanations of Dobet and the *Dobet* section or between those for Dobest and the *Dobest* section, because the terms Dobet and Dobest have no one meaning which those sections can dramatize" (op. cit., p. 36).

consider the second view according to which Dowel, Dobet and Dobest as the main divisions of the *Vita* correspond to the Purgative, Illuminative and Unitive Ways as successive "moments" of the soul's mystic progress, we should have less difficulty in accepting it as being, to a certain extent, more relevant to the actual development of the poem. This theory, however, provides, I think, only in part a solution to the problem of structure. For, while there can be no doubt that a process of purification and illumination takes place in the *Vita,* there is no clear evidence of a subsequent third stage of "mystic union" being achieved therein.[24] True, there are elements suggestive of an intense aspiration for the unitive condition of the soul, just as there are, especially in *Dobet* and *Dobest,* many visions of a supernatural nature. But, although much emphasis is put on the means necessary to achieve such a final goal, the poem does not contain a direct, total vision of God, as one would expect if the "triad" were applied by the poet in its entirety. The conclusion I can derive from a personal experience of the poem is that neither of the above triune concepts could be applied so consistently and so thoroughly as to furnish the keys to a definitive explanation of the *Vita's* structure. Furthermore, a blending of the two sets of correspondences would do little, I feel, to clarify or eliminate completely the manifest complexities of the poem.[25] Perhaps the truth is that Langland's mind was alien to any systematization and that all attempts in this direction will never prove completely satisfactory. Summing up this brief discussion, I venture to suggest that while threefold concepts such as that of Active, Contemplative and Mixed Lives, or

24. Fr. Dunning indirectly recognizes this when, having reviewed briefly the first two phases of the spiritual life, he notes: "Then, instead of leading us on to the third stage of the spiritual life, as do Rolle and Hilton, Tauler and Suso, the mystical stage in which the Holy Ghost works unimpeded in the soul, the poet, in the *Vita de Dobest,* quietly turns—as the definitions of Wit and Clergye had foreshadowed—to the third objective state, the life of prelates" (art. cit., p. 237).

25. Professor Donaldson's remark in this respect sounds sensibly empirical, following as it does soon after his own suggestion that the *Vita* should be seen as being based simultaneously on two ideas (above p. 89): "If this sort of interpretation seems too complicated, one can only answer, then so is *Piers Plowman*" (op. cit., p. 159).

that of Purgative, Illuminative and Unitive Ways remain, in their strict sequentiality, external to the actual organization of the poem, they may serve to illuminate, though in a limited way, some important aspects of Langland's conceptions—the conceptions he wanted to embody in Dowel, Dobet, and Dobest.[26]

If, on the other hand, we insist on searching for a pattern which could provide some unifying characteristics for the second part of *Piers Plowman,* a constant element which, in spite of the apparent discrepancies, could moreover help us to perceive the total unity of the poem,[27] it should not be so difficult to see it in the life of the Dreamer himself. I believe, in agreement with some recent critics, that by taking as the organizing principle of the *Vita* the story of the Dreamer and of his progress in the spiritual life, and by considering it in its main turning points, our effort at comprehension will be more fruitful.[28] And here, I should suggest, a comparison of the *Vita* with Dante's *Purgatorio* will be revealing and opportune, no matter how great the unavoidable differences.

I propose to attempt such a comparison following, however, a brief resumé of the various Passus in their relevant aspects.

Putting to one side the undeniable complexities with which every

26. My conclusion echoes that of S. S. Hussey, who also holds that "neither triad . . . nor a combination of the two is completely satisfactory as a definition of Dowel, Dobet and Dobest . . ." ("Langland, Hilton and the Three Lives", *RES,* vii, 1956, p. 146). I do not agree, however, with what seems to be Mr. Hussey's outright rejection of the triads.

27. I intend this as referring to both *Visio* and *Vita.* One is reminded at this point of Professor G. Kane's apposite observation that ". . . to describe *Piers Plowman* as planless is to ascribe an unlikely stupidity to a man otherwise highly intelligent; to argue that it is well or carefully planned is to fly in the face of the poem itself. The fact is that the one quality not to be found in *Piers Plowman* is system in the modern sense of the word" (op. cit., p. 247).

28. See e.g. Lawlor, op. cit., p. 306. This view is held also by J. F. Adams, in an interesting article on *"Piers Plowman* and the Three Ages of Man", *J.E.G.P.,* LXI (Jan. 1962), pp. 23-41. "The orientation of the poem," he writes, "the center which holds it together, is this embodiment in the Dreamer of the life of man. Dowel, Dobet, and Dobest provide nodes of meaning about which cluster a variety of elements significant to each stage of his progress. Unity is provided through the central intelligence of the Dreamer, in much the same way that Christian forms the center of *Pilgrim's Progress"* (ibid., p. 26).

reader of the *Vita* is confronted, we can follow the Dreamer's progress in its main thread of development. The poet in Passus VIII shows us the character Will wandering about in search of Dowel, that is the kind of higher life of which he became aware in the final dream of the *Visio*. It is Christian perfection he seeks after, and failing to see a living example of it in two Franciscan friars whom he has questioned, he turns to the world of discourse, thus initiating a kind of "introspective inquiry as to the degrees of right living".[29] During this first phase of his search Will gets involved in long discussions with Thought, Wit, Study, Clergy, and Scripture. The first two are personified intellectual faculties, almost a projection of his own mind, while the remainder appear as personifications of concepts of religious or, generally, academic learning, entities whose import is at one and the same time both simple and complex.[30] All of them, according to their abstract nature, give Will nothing but theoretical definitions of Dowel, Dobet and Dobest (Passus VIII, IX, X, beginning of XI). These definitions, centering roughly around the concepts of Active Life, the Religious Life, and the Life of Prelates—with an illustration of the necessary virtues that should accompany and qualify each of these states—although they say much that is true from an objective point of view, remain external means of knowledge: they are no help for an intimate adhesion to the ascetical living required for personal salvation. In the course of this internal *débat,* the Dreamer, bogged down by intellectual pride and dialectical argument, is tossed about from one character to another, and, failing to get unequivocal answers to his queries, is driven into a state of increasing bafflement and consequent despondency:

29. G. Hall Gerould, "The Structural Integrity of *Piers Plowman*" in *Studies in Philology*, XLV (Jan. 1948), p. 63.
30. I am fully aware of the difficulty of defining these terms. Cf. Dunning (*The A Text,* p. 173) who refers to them as "personified abstractions". Coghill (Introduction to Wells' *Translation of Piers Plowman into Modern English*, London 1935, p. xxi) calls them "ghostly informants", while Lawlor, op. cit., p. 86 ff., echoing Chambers, sees them as "Authorities". I should emphasize that the function of these personifications is more important than any disputable nomenclature. See R. W. Frank, op. cit., pp. 49-59; Robertson and Huppé, op. cit., p. 104 ff.

"This is a longe lessoun", quod I, "and litel am I the wyser;
Where Dowel is, or Dobet derkelich ye shewen;
Many tales ye tellen that Theologye lerneth;
And that I man made was and my name yentred
In the legende of lyf longe er I were,
Or elles vnwritten for somme wikkednesse as holywrit wytnes-
    seth,
Nemo ascendit ad celum, nisi qui de celo descendit.
I leue it wel," quod I, "bi owre lorde and on no letterure
    bettere.
For Salamon the sage that Sapience taughte,

. . . .

He demed wel and wysely as holy writte telleth.
Aristotle and he who wissed men bettere?

. . . .

And al holicherche holdeth hem both ydampned!"

                                    (B, X, 372-79; 382-3; 386)

["This is a long lesson," I said, "and I am little the wiser;
About where Do-well abides, or Do-better your directions are
    not clear—
You only tell me and teach me about Theology;
And that I was made man and my name entered
In the book of life long before I existed,
Or else was unwritten for some wickedness of mine as holy
    writ bears witness,
*No man has ascended up to Heaven, but that he came down
    from Heaven,*
I well believe it," I said, "on our Lord's word and on no
    other doctrine.
For Solomon the sage, who taught wisdom,

. . . .

Judged well and wisely as holy writ says.
Who taught men better than Aristotle and he?

. . . .

And yet the whole Church holds both to be damned!"]

Disappointed by a purely intellectual approach to the godly life,

Will concludes the first stage of his quest by condemning learning as a hindrance to salvation and by falling into the error of predestination.

Disoriented and disheartened, the Dreamer now drifts from his normal dream into a deeper oblivion in which he is carried away by the goddess Fortune to the "londe of Longynge" where, falling prey to *Concupiscencia carnis, Lust-of-the-eyes* and *Pryde-of-parfyte-lyuynge,* he abandons his pursuit of knowledge and virtue. The new forces of temptation, says Will:

> folwed me fourty wynter and a fyfte more,
> That of Dowel ne Dobet no deyntee me ne thoughte;
> I had no lykynge, leue me if the leste of hem aughte to knowe.
>
> (B, XI, 46-8)
>
> [followed me for forty years and a few more,
> So that I rated Do-well and Do-better of no importance,
> And had no desire, believe me if you will, to know anything
> about them.]

But when old age and poverty overtake him, Will, disillusioned by the world, begins again to ponder his own eternal salvation, and doubts whether he will be "chosen" or not at the final reckoning. Encouraged by the words of a new interlocutor, Trajan the Roman Emperor, who proclaims that he was released from Hell owing to simple love and righteousness, our Dreamer brings himself anew to discard the value of learning, and to rely purely on good faith and trust in divine mercy. But no sooner does he resume his quest for Do-well, than he suffers a new setback brought about by his usual bent for disputation. In a second inner dream Will is led by Kind (Nature)

> on a mountaigne that Myderlerd hyghte as me tho thoughte,
> I was fette forth by ensaumples to knowe,
> Thorough eche a creature and Kynde my creatoure to louye.
>
> (B, XI, 315-17)
>
> [on a mountain that was called Middle Earth, as it seemed
> to me,

I was led forth and shown by the example of each creature
    and Nature
How to love my Creator.]

Here he sees how the whole animal creation is ruled by a marvel-
lous Reason,[31] whereas only mankind is left to behave wickedly.
Will rebels against the manifest discrepancy and promptly re-
proaches Reason, indirectly criticizing even God. The strong
rebuke he earns from Reason for foolishly questioning the ways of
God, finally cures the Dreamer of his intellectual pride, and
humbles him so that he realizes and accepts man's innate feebleness. Presently our searcher returns to the stream of the main
vision and finds at his side Ymagynatif, a higher faculty of the
mind, with whose help he ponders on all that has gone before,
and thus benefits from his past experiences.[32] The intervention of
Imaginative (Passus XII) is clearly a resolution of the previous
confusions and uncertainties. Through it the Dreamer learns that
it is not expedient to lose oneself in idle theological inquiries, but
that the Christian life must be lived rather than be investigated, as
Study had warned him earlier (X, 132-34). Another important
lesson imparted to Will is the correction of his former views
concerning the value of Learning. It cannot be condemned outright, for although it entails a greater responsibility on the part of
the learned, if practised in the right spirit, it can be a useful and
valid means of salvation. Rather than criticize the clergy for the
discrepancy between the theory they profess and the life they lead
in practice,[33] or seek "after the whyes" (B, XII, 217) of everything in life, it is positively more important for the Dreamer—and
thus for each individual in general—to conform as best he can to

31. This passage runs from XI, 312 to 359. These lines undoubtedly
contain some of Langland's finest poetry; they represent an interlude of
pictorial vividness combined with a breath of vision which in the end rises
to a Lucretian pitch. Cf. Kane, op. cit., p. 202.

32. For an interesting analysis of Imaginative's function, see Lawlor,
op. cit., pp. 113-15.

33. We must remember that a great portion of these passus has been
devoted to a scathing satire against those ecclesiastics who betray the ideal
of true learning.

the moral law, to pursue a life of righteousness in humble faith, hope, and, above all, in a spirit of charity. Conscious of his own limitations, man can advance on the path of perfection only if assisted by Grace, a supernatural gift from God, which is above "Clergye" and "kynde witte" (XII, 61-71).

Through an unending series of debates marked by frequent pitfalls and setbacks, Will's introspection has led him to a deeper understanding of himself—that self-knowledge which is the indispensable premise for any real progress in the spiritual life. At the same time it has given him a clearer sense of values in his quest for the way to salvation.[34] As Professor Dunning has appropriately put it: "the diversity of our human faculties, the multiplicity of affections, the perpetual mobility of the mind are elements which must be understood if one wishes to control them".[35] The most significant result of this process of self-clarification which has taken place in Passus VIII-XII is the realization on the part of the protagonist of the necessity of practising the good he has been inquiring about. And at last we see him stepping into the high road of personal reform in a positive effort to follow the ascetical virtues. At the beginning of Passus XIII the fulfilment of his new resolution is encouraged by the reappearance on the scene of the moral power that enables Will to put into effect what he has learr'ʼ ᵗhe hard way:

I lay down longe in this thoughte and atte laste I slepte
And, as Cryste wolde, there come Conscience to conforte me
    that tyme . . .

(lines 21-22)

[Thinking thus, I lay down for a long time and at last I slept,
And, as Christ willed, Conscience came to comfort me then.]

Significantly, side by side with Conscience, Patience (here identified

---

34. "Multi multa sciunt et seipsos nesciunt", Scripture had warned earlier (cf. B, XI, 3-5), and a seemingly unidentified speaker urged Will to reflect on "Melius est scrutari scelera nostra, quam naturas rerum" (ibid., 223).
35. "The Structure of the B Text", RES, vii, p. 226.

with humility) appears to strengthen him further.[36] This basic Christian virtue, without which no genuine proficiency in the inner life is possible, has, incidentally, been inculcated repeatedly through the several rebukes suffered by the Dreamer throughout the preceding visions. Assisted by these two guides—"like the dream itself, they are real graces given to him by God"[37]—our hero can start anew on his pilgrimage.

The cursory analysis of this first part of the *Vita De Dowel* allows, I would suggest, a significant comparison with the first major division of the *Commedia's* second canticle. When due allowance has been made for the quite obvious differences in the actual narrative, general atmosphere, and characterization, if we take into consideration the true, deeper meaning of the Dreamer's experience up to this point and that recounted of the Pilgrim in Ante-Purgatory, striking points of similarity may be pointed out. On the whole, what takes place at this stage in both poems can be considered the allegorical representation of that initial phase of the spiritual life in which the human soul striving for moral liberty and perfection, after the negative experience of sin, acquires a clearer awareness of the duties—and hardships—which its new condition demands. Although with Dante the actual "figuration" of such a condition is realized mainly by means of a tense symbolism, whereas in Langland it is revealed through the resolution of a mental conflict, certain coinciding aspects can easily be discerned. First, there is, common to both, a general sense of bewilderment, a widespread feeling of uncertainty and confusion, characteristic of the soul in search of a firm footing in the newly chosen path leading to Christian perfection. In Dante's Ante-Purgatory this state of mind is rendered, for instance, by the sensation of vast solitude which dominates the landscape and surrounds two lonely pilgrims in search of their way:

36. Cf. D. C. Fowler, *Piers Plowman: Literary Relations of the A and B Texts,* Univ. of Washington Press 1961, p. 83. See also Robertson and Huppé, op. cit., pp. 160-61.
37. J. F. Goodridge, op. cit., p. 35.

Noi andavam per lo solingo piano
com'uom che torna a la perduta strada,
che infino ad essa li pare ire in vano.[38]

(*Purg.*, I, 118-20)

[We made our way over the lonely plain,
like one who returns to the road he has lost
and, till he finds it, seems to himself to go in vain.]

or by the evident disorientation pervading the souls who have just
disembarked on the shore of Purgatory:

La turba che rimase lì, selvaggia
parea del loco, rimirando intorno
come colui che nove cose assaggia.

(*Purg.*, II, 52-4)

[The crowd that remained there seemed strange to the place,
gazing about like those that make trial of things new.]

Indeed, the condition of the groups of spirits encountered in Ante-
Purgatory—a condition shared intimately by the wandering pilgrims[39]—that is of those who, as late repentants or excommuni-
cates, are outside the Church, and not yet admitted to the world
of active expiation and redemptive grace, is, on the whole, highly
suggestive of an intermediate stage of uncertainty in the inner life.
It lies between the determination to acquire the positive good and
a definite orientation towards it. In Langland the same mood is
conveyed not symbolically, but perhaps with a more genuine 'liter-
alness' throughout most of the *Dowel* section, by the perplexities,
the frustrations, the hesitant doubtings of a Dreamer wrestling

38. See also e.g. VIII, 1-6. Commenting on the above lines (I, 118-20)
A. Momigliano admittedly notes: "Il viaggio nel Purgatorio significa *prima
smarrimento dello spirito che cerca la via della liberazione morale,* poi
faticosa disciplina, infine conquista della meta agognata" ["The journey
through Purgatory signifies first the bewilderment of the human spirit in
search of the path of moral freedom, then laborious discipline, and lastly
the arrival at the keenly desired goal"] (op. cit., p. 270; italics mine).
39. "Noi siam peregrin come voi siete" ["We are strangers like your-
selves"] Virgil says to them (ibid., 63).

with the problems posed by his search for some sure pointers to
the highway to Truth. It is especially in the waking interludes that
the feeling is expressed, and sometimes in a poignant manner:

> And thus I went wide-where walking mine one,
> By a wilde wildernesse and bi a wode-side.
> (B, VIII, 62-3)
> Thanne Scripture scorned me and a skile tolde,
> And lakked me in Latyne and lighte by me she sette,
> And seyde, *"multi multa sciunt, et seipsos nesciunt."*
> Tho wepte I for wo and wratth of her speche,
> And in synkyng wratth wex I aslepe.
> (B, XI, 1-5)
> And I awaked there-with witles nerehande,
> And as a freke that fre were forth gan I walke
> In manere of a mendynaunt many a yere after ...
> (B, XIII, 1-3)
> [And thus I went far and wide walking alone,
> In a wild wilderness and by a wooded place.]

> [Then Scripture poured scorn on me and gave her reasons,
> And blamed me in Latin and had a poor opinion of me,
> And said *"There are many who know much, but themselves
>   they do not know."*
> Then I wept in woe and was angered by her speech,
> And as I drowsed I fell asleep in a wrathful mood.]

> [And with that I awaked, nearly out of my mind,
> And as a man who was free I began to walk forth,
> In the manner of a mendicant—for many a year after ...]

True, we could hardly hear the Pilgrim of Purgatory express
weariness with his journey in such utterances of rueful resignation
—verging almost on despondency—as those in which the Dreamer
of the *Vita* gives vent to his having to endure the unpleasant
reality of man's "unreasonableness":

Tho caughte I coloure anon and comsed to ben aschamed,
And awaked ther-with; wo was me thanne
That I in meteles ne myghte more haue yknowen.
And thanne seyde I to my-self and chidde that tyme;
"Now I wote what Dowel is," quod I, "by dere god, as me
    thinketh."
And as I caste vp myn eyghen one loked on me and axed
Of me, what thinge it were? "ywisse, sire", I seide,
"To se moche and suffre more certes", quod I, "is Dowel!"
                                               (B, XI, 395-402)
[Then at once I blushed and began to be ashamed,
And with that I awoke; I was woeful then
That in my dreams did not learn even more.
And then I took thought and found fault with myself:
"Now I know what Do-well is," I said, "by dear God, as it
    seems to me."
And as I cast up my eyes someone looked at me and asked
Of me, what thing it was. "Indeed, sir," I said,
"Most certainly," I said, "Do-well means to see much and
    suffer even more!"]

But lines such as these contained in Ymagynatyf's elegiac medi-
tation on Will's past experience:

I have folwed the in feithe this fyue and fourty wyntre,
And many tymes haue moeued the to thinke on thine ende,
And how fele fer yeres are faren and so fewe to come . . .
                                               (B, XII, 3-6)
[I have followed you in the path of faith these five and forty
    winters,
And have many times moved you to think of your end,
And of all the years that are gone and the few that remain . . .]

besides communicating "at one and the same time the length of
years and the absence of definite purpose",[40] poignantly convey
the insistent character of our preoccupation with our uncertain

40. Lawlor, op. cit., p. 224.

journey such as we have also seen in the above verse of Dante.[41] In the second place, it must be noted that in the midst of all this disorientation, and actually occasioned by it, there have been some firm points clearly established for both Pilgrim and Dreamer, such as the inexorable necessity to accept one's own personal responsibility in facing the demands of right living on the one hand, and the uncompromising acceptance of the Law, on the other— first on the level of natural morality, and consequently on that of Christian belief.[42] Just as Dante becomes aware of this essential condition in his encounter with the unflinching Guardian of Purgatory, so Will's various interlocutors constantly hammer home for him the compelling necessity to face up to moral duty, the fulfilment of which is all the more urgent the more he dallies.

> "Dowel, my friend, is to don as lawe techeth."
>
> (B, IX, 199)
>
> ["Do-well, my friend, is to do as the law teaches."]

says Wit, while Lady Study reiterates that disputation is pointless and curses him who indulges in it. It is no use looking for fine distinctions between Do-well and Do-better

> But if he lyue in the lyf that longeth to Dowel;
> For I dar ben his bolde borgh that Dobet wil he neuere,
> Theigh Dobest drawe on hym day after other.
>
> (B, X, 132-34)

---

41. Compare with this also the following meditative lines:
   ... ché perder tempo a chi più sa più spiace.

   (*Purg.*, III, 78)

and
   ... vassene il tempo e l'uom non se n'avvede.

   (*Purg.*, IV, 9)

   [... for loss of time most grieves him that knows best.]
   [... the time passes and one is not aware.]
They are similar in tone with the last quoted from Langland.

42. By and large most of the definitions of Dowel centre on the notion of those virtues that pertain to natural morality as a preliminary step towards the higher Christian spirituality. See, for instance, Thought's definition of Dowel in B, VIII, 78-83; Wit's speech on man's nature in B, IX, 1-24; or the same Faculty talking of true wedlock, B, IX, 107-17.

[Unless he lives the life that belongs to Do-well;
For I am prepared to pledge my life that he will never Do-
    better,
Although Do-best keep tugging at him day after day.]

A third, all-important element present in both poems at this stage
of the two protagonists' spiritual development, and closely con-
necting them, is the far-reaching realization that in his effort to
acquire Truth man can and must avail himself of—and use properly
—the natural means of knowledge, although only the intervention
of supernatural grace can help us to achieve perfection. For Dante
Virgil is the *lumen naturale* which, in spite of limitations and
insufficiencies of its guiding power, is always there to assist and
encourage us on the steep road of self-comprehension and moral
reform. And such a role is played by Virgil all along the path—
the long climb almost to the top of the Mount. The same function,
I believe, is fulfilled by the various rational faculties in their
relation with Will the Dreamer all through the *Dowel* section.
Notwithstanding the obvious inadequacy of their teachings, in the
long run theirs is a positive contribution not only to the intellectual
enlightenment of Will, but also to his moral education. Though
his rebellious spirit and overweening concern with himself make
his advancement slower and more painfully circuitous—and therefore more dramatic—the Dreamer comes to accept the validity of
true learning and is, despite the seemingly dispersive plurality of
these faculties, prepared to meet again Conscience and Patience—
the practical virtues which will assist him in a more concrete
fashion to pursue the ascetical life.[43] Finally, if to the various
aspects already considered we add those instances of temporary
flagging or those 'moments' of crisis that may divert one perilously

43. H. W. Wells saw the problem in this light when he wrote: "Clearly
each character has something to contribute to the Pilgrim's growing knowledge of his life's journey. Each represents a progressive stage in his education" (op. cit., p. 133). But he failed, as many others have failed, to stress
further and with due emphasis this connection between what we may call
"ethics" and "ascesis". See also, R. W. Frank, op. cit., pp. 65-7.

from the pursuit of the set goal,[44] we can recognize a significant correspondence of motifs that will, ultimately, bespeak an essential similarity from the allegorical point of view between *Antipurgatorio* and the *Dowel* section. This similarity can be further strengthened and seen more completely by referring to the presence in both poets of Humility, the basic Christian virtue which is enjoined on Dante at the outset—and to which Will is led inescapably towards the end—and which constitutes the *sine qua non* for success in the spiritual life.[45] As a representation of the soul's journey in a delicate moment of preparation for the promised land—a moment filled with pitfalls and hope, temptations and impulses of liberation from them—the parts of the two poems we have just considered can be said to reveal not only a thematic analogy but also a considerable amount of structural parallelism.

Such elements of similarity cannot be expected, however, to be present consistently throughout, although some important aspects

44. The temptations experienced both by Pilgrim and Dreamer underline dramatically this aspect. Obviously the spiritual oblivion in which Will falls prey to Fortune is different from the temptation scene in the Valley of Princes (see above p. 80). The fascination of the enchantress's song has its equivalent in the words of *Concupiscencia carnis*:

"Thow art yonge and yepe and hast yeres ynowe,
Forto lyue longe and ladyes to louye;
And in this myroure thow myghte se myrthes ful manye,
That leden the wil to lykynge al thi lyf-tyme."
(B, XI, 17-20)
["You are young and vigorous and have many years before you,
To live long and love women;
And in this mirror you may see unending delights
That lead the will towards sensual pleasure all your life-time."]
And when soon after Fortune herself adds (line 25):
"The freke that folwed my wille failled neuere blisse."
["The man who followed my will never wanted for joy."]
the similarity could not be more striking between this and the last captivating words of the Siren:
... e qual meco s'ausa,
rado sen parte; sì tutto l'appago.
(*Purg.*, XIX, 23-4)
[... and he who dwells with me
rarely departs, so wholly I content him.]
45. Perhaps we should note that Langland in his usual way of providing "foretastes" has adumbrated the basic significance of humility towards the end of Passus X.

of the other Passus of the *Vita* can be revealingly connected with
the *Purgatorio*. In the second main vision of *Dowel* (Books
XIII-XIV), the Dreamer, strengthened by Conscience, seems at
last to step forward from theoretical inquiry into practice of the
virtues which enable him to make some progress towards sancti-
fication. The first important virtue implanted in him is Patience,[46]
here personified by a poor pilgrim who shares with Will the sour
food of *agite penitenciam* at the dinner feast called by Conscience.
Armed with patience Will can endure witnessing a concrete instance of the clergy's crass worldliness, embodied in the fat gluttonous friar who gorges himself with dainty food and drink while
glibly pontificating on theology (XIII, 21-110). The masterly comedy of the banquet scene, however, serves not only to expose
clerical gluttony and hypocrisy, but to reaffirm the dignity of
learning, an ideal blatantly betrayed on the one side and re-estab-
lished on the other. It is Clergye, the other allegorical guest of the
party, after all, who pleads with Conscience and Patience for the
recognition of learning's value. Although limited, learning, when
pursued in the right subordinate spirit, can usefully join with the
superior virtues in order to achieve Dowel. And it is Clergye,
characteristically, who, by recognizing his limitations, opens the
widest avenue of boundless Love, infinite and superior to all
sciences:

> For one Pieres the Ploughman hath impugned vs alle,
> And sette alle sciences at a soppe saue loue one,
> And no tixte ne taketh to meyntene his cause,
> But *dilige deum* and *domine, quis habitabit,* &c.
> And seith that Dowel and Dobet aren two infinites,

---

46. Most commentators of *Piers Plowman* gloss the meaning of Patience
by referring to the various scriptural sources and to the definitions of the
Fathers. See e.g. Robertson and Huppé, *Piers Plowman and Scriptural
Tradition,* cit., pp. 164-5. The most appropriate references, however, seem
to me those made by Dunning who quotes Gregory the Great and Aquinas.
"Patience," he writes, "is put forward as the virtue which will render
Reason's teaching stable and make progress along the road to Truth pos-
sible" ("B Structure", *RES,* vii, p. 236, note 1).

Whiche infinites, with a feith fynden oute Dobest,
Which shal saue mannes soule; thus seith Piers the Ploughman.
(B, XIII, 123-29)
[For a certain Piers the Ploughman has accused us all,
And reckoned all knowledge as not worth a sop, except Love
    alone,
And depends on no other text to support his cause
But *Love God* and *Lord, who shall dwell in thy tabernacle*, etc.
He says that Do-well and Do-better are two absolutes,
Which absolutes discover Do-best by means of faith,
And which shall save man's soul; so says Piers the
    Ploughman.]

With the mention of Piers and the prophetic utterance attributed
to him by Clergye, the *Vita* and the whole poem come to a crucial
turning point, for the figure of the humble Ploughman of the
Visio is, almost unexpectedly, presented as mysteriously transformed and possessing the gifts of grace together with the secret
of the authentic spiritual life,[47] while the triad Dowel, Dobet and
Dobest is seen to reach out to a dimension of infinity. True to his
purpose and nature, however, the poet does not let Piers's statement appear to be the mere expression of a distant, rarefied ideal-
ism, but brings into play once again the abstract entities assisting
the Dreamer at this moment of his progress in wisdom, to illustrate the practical import of the message: "the truth of Love and
its unlimited power".[48] Fittingly it is Patience who perceives the
meaning of those words more deeply than Learning (Clergye) and
Conscience, and it is he who, in the discussion which follows,
defines Dowel, Dobet and Dobest as *Disce, Doce, Dilige inimicos,*
concentrating on this last most difficult but essential command:
to love one's enemy. When man obeys the law of love in a spirit

47. D. C. Fowler maintains that Piers has not actually spoken those
words, and that the author of the B text made use of the popularity of
Piers already established by the A text (op. cit., pp. 89-90). This, however,
does not detract in any way from the idealization the B poet assigns to
Piers from now on.
48. J. Lawlor, op. cit., p. 120.

of patient endurance, he is well on the way towards succeeding in the practice of Christian virtue, for *Caritas nichil timet* and *Pacientes vincunt* (B, XIII, 135-72). Conscience agrees wholeheartedly with Patience's conclusion, and speaking for Clergye also, proclaims:

"If Pacience be owre partyng felawe and pryue with vs bothe,
There nys wo in this worlde that we ne shulde amende,
And confourmen kynges to pees and al kynnes londes,
Sarasens and Surre and so forth alle the Iewes
Turne in-to the trew feithe and in-til one byleue."

(B, XIII, 206-10)

["If Patience were our travelling companion and intimate with us both,
There is no evil in this world that we could not put right,
And we would make peace between kings and nations of every kind,
And convert to the one true faith and creed
Saracens and Syrians and indeed all the Jews."]

Yet no sooner are we, with the Dreamer, confirmed in the need to pursue such an ideal and, armed with "Sobrete, and symple-speche and sothfaste byleue" (ibid., 217), try to follow the dictates of Conscience and Patience in order to proceed onwards, than we are faced anew with the reality of the human condition. On resuming the pilgrimage to Truth we meet with *Haukyn Actiua Vita*. In this composite figure, in fact, the author presents, with his typically incisive sense of the actual, another devastating picture of mankind's shortcomings and fallibility. Haukyn sums up in himself the majority of laymen who, while concerning themselves excessively with the purveyance of material welfare, delude themselves with the notion that they are observing the tenets of the faith by paying lip-service to its requirements. Haukyn's boisterous recitation of the benefits conferred by him on society cannot then be a claim to righteousness. On closer scrutiny his coat appears

... fouler by felefolde than it firste semed.

(B, XIII, 320)

[... many times filthier than it seemed at first.]

and for the second time in the poem, the full array of the Deadly
Sins is marshalled for us as, almost inevitably, affecting the greater
part of those engaged in the active world. The obvious way to
cleanse the soiled coat of sinful man is by resort to penance and
the traditional acts of the Church's sacraments. *Cordis contricio,
Oris confessio, Satisfactio* are slowly, but efficaciously, enjoined
upon Haukyn by Conscience (B, XIV, 1-27). Yet, while the healing
power of confession and penance remains the surest means of
regaining "the fairness of the baptismal garment" (cf. XIV, 24),
good of a more positive kind must be performed. The fruitfulness
of contrition is enhanced by the full acceptance of "patient poverty", of the doctrine of *ne solliciti sitis* in all its implications, and
of obedience to the law of love—all combined in a new, eloquent
synthesis of the central message contained in Christ's Gospel for
men.[49] From the dependence on the Creator's providence, with
Pater noster—fiat voluntas tua, through the renewed stressing of
the nature of poverty and its incomparable merits over against
the dangers of riches,[50] to the solemn and almost joyous ringing of
Beati pauperes, quoniam ipsorum est regnum celorum—Patience's
speech, which occupies most of Passus XIV, painstakingly brings
home to the Haukyns of this world the real spirit and substance of

49. The relationship between penance, patient poverty, and the doctrine
of *ne solliciti sitis,* was, as many commentators have pointed out, common
teaching of the moralists and theologians in Langland's time. But, as R. W.
Frank pointedly notes: "The particular combination of these doctrines in
the poem and the emphasis they receive is the poet's own creation" (op. cit.,
p. 75).

50. This point is brought out by Langland through a second listing of the
Deadly Sins which attack more easily men of wealth than the poor. The
latter shall win salvation, however, only when they have accepted and practised the right spirit of poverty (cf. B, XIV, 201-272).

the living faith.[51] With a further realization of the divergence existing between the ideal of perfection—harsh yet attainable— and the actual, all too common state of sinfulness, the Visio of *Dowel* comes to an end as Haukyn

> ... cryde mercye faste,
> And wepte and weyled, and there-with I awaked.
>
> (B, XIV, 331-32)
>
> [... cried earnestly for mercy,
> And wept and wailed, and with that I awoke.]

On the whole the second part of *Dowel* has marked an important step forward in the Dreamer's pilgrimage. Through the lessons of Conscience and Patience together with the dissipation of Haukyn's moral disorder, two main aspects of Christian life have been inculcated in him, both theoretically and practically: penance and the active pursuit of the evangelical counsels. In this respect the coincidence with the second section of the *Purgatorio* appears obvious, since it is here that the Pilgrim of the *Commedia* enters decisively upon the ground of active penance, as we saw earlier,[52] by first performing the sacramental acts, and then embarking on a thorough confrontation with the Seven Sins through the slow and painful ascent of the mountain cornices. Certainly the disproportion in the number of books allotted by each poet to the treatment of the Sins[53] could not be more striking. And, of course, it should be noted that *Activa Vita's* besmeared coat forms not just a repetition, but an adaptation and a completion of the confession scene in Passus V, where a more orderly and regular list of the vices was displayed. But no matter how great the difference in "quantity", it is worth noting that what we may call a second

---

51. Regarding the eulogy of the Beatitudes at this point in the poem, D. C. Fowler's remark is worth noting: "... the twentieth-century reader, who perhaps has tired of hearing modern literary critics praise the 'beauty' of the Sermon on the Mount, may feel refreshed to discover that our poet understands its meaning" (op. cit., p. 97).

52. See above, pp. 81-2.

53. Cantos X-XXVI in Dante's *Purgatorio*.

analysis of sin in both poems is here carried out through examples
of living humanity, portrayed by Dante in a rich and varied series
of historical and legendary figures, but concentrated by Langland
in the lowly, un-heroic personality of Haukyn, whose relative
anonymity does not destroy but rather enhances the realistic
characterization of a multiform and strangely familiar picture of
general mankind. Moreover, the all-important feature which bespeaks a quasi-identical purpose and direction at this particular
stage both in the *Vita* and in the *Purgatorio* is the strict association
of the repentance motif with the call to contemplate and practise
the ascetical virtues, which are identified in both poets with the
Beatitudes of the New Law. Thus, as in Patience's passionate
discourse, so at the end of each cornice of Purgatory there resounds
the praise of a Beatitude underlying and completing, as it were,
every step of the way of purgation. Admittedly, whereas in Dante
not only *Beati pauperes spiritu* (*Purg.*, XII, 110) but the whole
series of the counsels occur in an organic and perfect balance,
each corresponding to its counter vice,[54] in Langland the stress
is mainly laid on the virtue of patient poverty. Nevertheless, it
must be recognized that, however comprehensive and evenly dis-
posed, Dante's is but a catalogue of Benedictions which punctuate
the ascent with a sweetly poetic appeal; Langland, instead,
seems to have gathered the whole spirit of the Sermon of the
Mount into a single, all-embracing virtue which goes to the very
heart of the genuine Christian life—although he does this in a
comparatively more prosaic tone, which betrays the poet's practical concern and "sermonizing" attitude. This does not mean that
the section of the *Vita* we are considering in relation to the *Purgatorio* is devoid of poetical beauty or authentic imagination. Haukyn

54. For instance, *Beati misericordes* and *Godi tu che vinci* are heard after
crossing the terrace of the Wrathful (*Purg.*, XV, 38-9). Both, incidentally,
seem to echo *pacientes vincunt*. *Beati pacifici* (XVII, 69); *Beati qui lugent*
(XIX, 50); and so forth up to *Beati mundo corde* following the purging of
the sin of Lust (XXVII, 8). All Beatitudes are sung by the Angel of the
cornice when the mark of each vice is erased from the Pilgrim's forehead,
thus pointing to virtues corrective of the seven sins. More than being
another feature of the poem's structural symmetry, the beatitudes resound
as an insistent, joyful invitation to advance farther and higher.

is one of Langland's most impressive and convincing creations and
Patience's praise of patient poverty often attains a highly lyrical
fervour. What, however, is necessary for us to indicate at this
point is the fact that we are confronted here with a similar phase
in the process of moral reform, in which man's soul, bending once
more over itself, acquires a deeper awareness of its infirmity, and
through the cleansing power of penance can look up once more
towards the not so distant horizon of perfection. This sentiment
pervades Purgatory, but is perhaps no better and no more eloquently epitomized than in the encounter of the Pilgrim with the
souls of the Covetous who are shedding from their heart the dross
of their once besetting sin: inordinate love of wealth and satisfaction of worldly ambitions, which now are recognized as utter
vanities:

> Com'io nel quinto giro fui dischiuso,
>   vidi gente per esso che piangea,
>   giacendo a terra tutta volta in giuso.
> *"Adhaesit pavimento anima mea"*
>   sentia dir lor con sì alti sospiri,
>   che la parola a pena s'intendea.

(Purg., XIX, 70-5)

[When I had come out in the open on the fifth round I saw
people along it who were weeping, all lying face downward
on the ground. *"Adhaesit pavimento anima mea"* I heard
them say with sighs so deep that the words could hardly be
distinguished.]

The spokesman for these spirits is, significantly, a Pope, Hadrian
V, who, while explaining the mode of their punishment, acknowledges repentantly the futility of human achievements, and the
delay they cause in the conversion to unperishable good:

> "Vidi che li non si quetava il core,
>   né più salir potiesi in quella vita;
>   per che di questa in me s'accese amore.
> . . . .

Sì come l'occhio nostro non s'aderse
in alto, fisso a le cose terrene,
così giustizia qui a terra il merse.
Come avarizia spense a ciascun bene
lo nostro amore, onde operar perdesi,
cosi giustizia qui stretti ne tene ..."

(ibid., 109-11; 118-23)

["I saw that there the heart was not at rest;
nor was it possible to mount higher in that life,
so that love of this was kindled in me.

. . . .

Just as our eyes, fixed on earthly things, did
not lift themselves on high, so justice here has sunk
them to the earth; as avarice quenched all our love
of good so that our labours were vain, so justice
here holds us fast ..."]

Hadrian V's is a "personal" story, but told as it is in collective terms, has an unmistakable universal resonance as well as a clear allegorical implication. In the general economy of Purgatory proper —the second section of the poem, that is, illustrating in the context of active penance how man strives to free his judgement and will —this episode brings into focus the tension ever present in the life of the Christian between earth-bound desires and the aspiration for a wholesome spiritual life. *Adhesit pavimento anima mea:* "my soul cleaveth to the dust" (Ps. 119:25): it is both a prayer and a recognition of failure. The whole episode of Haukyn—it is not hard to discern—is animated by the spirit of the same Psalm. Essentially, though in a more circumstantial and varied representation, the vision of *Activa Vita* sets forth the continual care, and yet the complete lack of proper satisfaction, which attends the acquisition and the possession of wealth or the attainment of worldly success. Haukyn may exhibit the full range of Deadly Sins, but in his confession the stress falls over and over again on covetousness, often allied with miserliness:

"So if I kydde any kyndenesse myn euen-cristene to helpe,
Vpon a cruel coueityse myn herte gan hange.
. . . .

Ne neuere penaunce perfourned ne *pater noster* seyde,
That my mynde ne was more on my gode, in a doute,
Than in the grace of god and his grete helpes:
   Vbi thesaurus tuus, ibi et cor tuum."
                                    (B, XIII, 390-1; 396-9)
["So if I showed any kindness in helping my fellow Christians,
My heart, however, clung only closer to cruel covetousness.
. . . .

Nor did I ever perform penance or say a pater noster
But that my mind was more troubled by thoughts of my goods
Than centred on the grace of God and his great mercies:
   For where your treasure is, there will your heart be also."]

And his growing awareness of his life having been spent in the
pursuit of what now appears inordinately wasteful (cf. Hadrian's
"whereby was action lost", line 122, above p. 112), rouses in
him a cry of contrition as deeply felt as that of the penitent on the
fifth ledge of Purgatory—and even louder:

"Allas!" quod Haukyn the actyf man tho "that after my
      Crystendome,
I ne hadde ben ded and doluen for Doweles sake!
So harde it is," quod Haukyn, "to lyue and to do synne.
Synne suweth vs euere" quod he and sori gan wexe,
And wepte water with his eyghen and weyled the tyme,
That euere he dede dede that dere god displesede;
Swowed and sobbed and syked ful ofte,
That euere he hadde londe or lordship ...
                                    (B, XIV, 320-27)
["Alas!" said Haukyn the active man, then "that after my
      baptism
I was not straightaway dead and buried, for Do-well's sake!
It is so painful," said he, "to live and keep on committing sin.

Sin pursues us all the time" he said and grew sad and sorry,
And he shed tears from his eyes and grieved for the days
That ever he did things which displeased his dear God;
Swooned and sobbed and sighed over and over again
Because he ever owned land and wielded authority.]

It is interesting to note also that just as Haukyn's spiritual regeneration depends not only on an act of genuine repentance but on
the willingness to accept and love positively the virtue of patient
poverty as well, so the contrite protestation to renounce worldly
vanity uttered by the Avaricious is followed by their invoking
examples of holy poverty and generosity. It is a pressing appeal to
cherish and practise the evangelical counsel, which reaches the
traveller of Purgatory as a corroboration of his spiritual reform.[55]

Furthermore, if we consider that the foundation of this experience of renewal is, in both poems, an act of obedient faith,
expressed in the Lord's Prayer—Dante hears it from the Proud,
the first group of penitent spirits, while it forms the opening of
Patience's speech[56]—it can be seen that there are many points of
contact between the two poets in their illustration of the repentance theme. It should not be amiss here to observe that while
Dante, the Pilgrim, remains constantly at the centre of the process
of purgation, perfectly balanced between the personal and the
universal, Langland's Dreamer seems somehow to disappear from
the scene. Only by remembering that, after all, the second vision
of *Dowel* takes place for his own benefit, too, can one appreciate
that the search does not cease to be a spiritual autobiography. For,
although the pilgrimage comes to embrace general mankind in the

55. See *Purg.*, XX, 19-33. The Virgin Mary, the virtuous Roman Fabri-
cius and St. Nicholas, are here mentioned as exemplars of poverty. It is a
sober, yet effective, exhortation which, admittedly, can hardly compare
with Patience's passionate eulogy of patient poverty.

56. B, XIV, 47-8: *"Pater noster . . . fiat voluntas tua"* is, in Langland's
typical way, a *lyflode* offered by Patience to Haukyn, and is referred to in
the context of the doctrine of *ne solliciti sitis*. In Dante, instead, we have a
periphrasis of the prayer recited by the penitent in a spirit of humility and
universal love for the living: cf. *Purg.*, XI, 1-24. It is only its presence—
from a structural viewpoint—that I want to stress.

person of Haukyn, Will the Dreamer is too intimately associated with him for us to assume that his presence is forgotten altogether.[57] Therefore we are not far from the truth in concluding that, with due allowance being made for differences in characterization and actual symmetry, *Dowel* in its main allegory is a worthy companion to a great portion of *Purgatorio*.

57. J. F. Goodridge (op. cit., p. 36) rightly remarks in this respect: "Later, at the beginning of Book XVI, when Will thanks Anima for his teaching, he adds these words: 'I shall always love you now, *for Haukyn's sake*' ... and values all he has learnt during his search, solely for the sake of Haukyn". Here the Dreamer is "too closely involved with Haukyn in the Argument to be aware of himself as a spectator".

CHAPTER 4

BEATRICE AND PIERS

We have seen that the purgatorial journey of the *Commedia* and the arduous quest of *Piers Plowman* have revealed, so far, a certain parallel in allegorical development. Through the conquest of sin and the purifying efficacy of sacramental grace the soul of man becomes worthy of being a member of the Church Militant. The attainment of this loftier level of spiritual life is portrayed in the *Purgatorio* in the visions of the Earthly Paradise, and in *Piers Plowman* it is shown in the visions of *Dobet* and *Dobest,* Passus XV-XVIII and XIX-XX respectively. Let us look briefly at the outlines of both treatments.

In Dante this charismatic process, a premonition of the supernatural revelations of Paradise, is enacted through the vision of a symbolical pageant—a true mystery play, displayed with a condensed allegory of conventional type, in which the Pilgrim is both spectator and participant. The sacred spectacle that unfolds in front of Dante's eyes is divided into two parts. The first is a solemn procession whose centre-piece is a Gryphon, image of Christ in His hypostatic union, driving the Chariot of the Church, surrounded on each side by dancing maidens, the three Theological and the four Cardinal Virtues. Seven candlesticks shed the rainbow-like light of the Holy Ghost's Gifts over the Chariot. This is preceded by twenty-four elders, crowned with lilies, representing the Books of the Old Testament, and is followed by four winged animals, the traditional emblematic figures of the New Testament Authors (Canto XXIX). It is Matelda,[1]

---

1. The interpretations of Matelda's "literal" and "allegorical" identity are as many and varied as the commentaries on the poem. The majority of commentators recognize in her the famous Countess of Canossa, by Dante transfigured here into the image or "type" of Active Life in the highest

una donna soletta che si gìa
   cantando ed iscegliendo fior da fiore
   ond'era dipinta tutta la sua via

                 (*Purg.,* XXVIII, 40-2)

[a lady all alone, who went singing and
culling flower from flower with which
all her way was painted]

who, after introducing the Pilgrim to the inalterable beauty of the
place, has directed him to contemplate the sacred representation
within which his moral recovery is to be completed. It is, in fact,
the historical and at the same time eternal Church that advances
to meet the repentant sinner, and reveals herself in the glory of
Christ's army before receiving him into her bosom. But the dispensation of sacramental union is performed through the sacerdotal
function of Beatrice, who now appears on the Chariot, in the full
splendour of her hallowed state. We have reached the focal point
of the whole *Commedia,* the encounter of Dante with his Beloved,
here transfigured in the "God-bearing Image".[2] Hailed with the
song *"Veni Sponsa de Libano"* and *"Benedictus Qui Venis",*
girt with the olive of true wisdom, and dressed with the colours of
the three theological virtues, Beatrice comes to assume the central
role of a liturgical rite, which develops with the sequence of the
Mass, and through which the final regeneration of Dante's spirit
can be effected. Gazing into her unveiled eyes Dante sees the light
of Christ reflected in them, in the intimate association of the
Redeemer with a sanctified human being:

e le mie luci, ancor poco sicure,
   vider Beatrice volta in su la fiera
   ch'è sola una persona in due nature.

Christian sense, or the symbol of *Sapientia* in the biblical sense. Her important function, at any rate, is to "prepare" for the "revelation" of Beatrice.
   2. Among the numerous "significations" of Beatrice at this central point
of the allegorical narrative, I find this the most appropriate and inclusive
one, suggested by D. L. Sayers in her commentary. Cf. op. cit., p. 311.

. . . .
Di penter sì mi punse ivi l'ortica,
  che di tutte altre cose qual mi torse
  più nel suo amor, più mi si fe' nemica.

. . . .
Come in lo specchio sol, non altrimenti
  la doppia fiera dentro vi raggiava,
  or con altri, or con altri reggimenti.
(Purg., XXXI, 79-81; 85-7; 121-3)

[and my eyes, still lacking confidence,
saw Beatrice turned toward the beast which is
one sole person in two natures.

. . . .
The nettle of remorse so stung me there
that of all other things that which had
most bent me to the love of it became for me the most hateful.

. . . .
Even like the sun in a mirror the twofold
beast shone within them, now with the one,
now with the other nature.]

The incarnation of Revealed Truth and repository of Christ's illuminating grace, Beatrice exercises also His power of judgement and forgiveness; faced once more with his past misdeeds, Dante acquires again full conscience of sin's horror and, purified by a baptismal immersion in the waters of Lethe and Eunoë, achieves spiritual wholeness. Before, however, being made

    puro e disposto a salire a le stelle
(Purg., XXXIII, 145)
    [pure and ready to mount to the stars]

he must enlarge the horizon of his individual salvation in order to come to the vision of universal redemption as ordained by Providence for all mankind. It is in the second part of the pageant that we are shown, by means of deeply symbolical movements, the essential moments of Christ's redemptive action, and the story of

the Church Militant from apostolic times to the poet's own day.
The procession of the Church now moves towards the Tree of
Knowledge, which, in its bareness, represents the fallen nature of
man after and because of Adam's sin. The Gryphon attaches the
Chariot-pole to it. The Tree immediately blossoms: as the Cross
enters temporal history, mankind is regenerated in a new life. But
when the Gryphon departs to re-enter Heaven, Beatrice, who, as
depository of the Word, is left to guard the Chariot, bids Dante
look attentively at the ensuing vision of the tragic events befalling
Christendom. An eagle descends impetuously on the cart and
shatters it, tearing at the same time the bark from the tree (the
Church harrassed by the persecutions of the Roman Emperors);
then a raving fox (Heresy) comes to the assault but is chased away
by Beatrice. Again there returns the eagle to perpetrate the corruption of the Church with the Donation of Constantine, followed by
a Dragon who does further damage with the rending of Schism,
until on the cart, now covered with the weeds of complete worldliness, appear the seven heads of the capital sins; and a Harlot
fornicating with a Giant will show the slavery of the Babylonian
captivity. The Christian believer, strengthened by the victory
secured through Christ's grace at the end of his expiatory course,
has been enabled to witness the ever-recurrent drama of the
Church, liable here below to suffer tribulations in the course of
time from within and without. The apocalyptic vision of the
Church's temporary reverses, revealing in a solemn and tragic
pantomime, as it were, how the two supreme Authorities of Christendom by their mutual jealousy and greed may thwart the divine
plan of Redemption, casts a shadow of gloom on the journey's
end. But a final word of assurance will confirm the poet's faith in
the ultimate triumph of God's justice. With enigmatic but resolute
words Beatrice prophesies the advent of a Deliverer, a "messo di
Dio" who

> . . . anciderà la fuia
> con quel gigante che con lei delinque.

(Purg., XXXIII, 44-5)

> [. . . shall slay the thievish woman
> and the giant who sins with her.]

Church and Empire, regenerated, will again guide mankind towards the fulfilment of its earthly as well as of its heavenly destiny. The mind's flight into total Truth and Love can now begin.

Turning now to the visions of *Dobet* and *Dobest* we soon become aware that of the two sections it is the former that realizes the deeper degree of spiritual fruition. In Passus XV (usually referred to as the Prologue to *Dobet*), the Dreamer meets in his sleep with *Anima,* in whom all the powers of Life, Mind, and Spirit coalesce. Through Anima's discourse, the longest in the *Vita,* Will acquires a more thorough understanding of the meaning of Charity, and a better appreciation of Learning's place in the good life. Priests and religious are vehemently attacked at great length for their disloyalty to those ideals. Soul's sermon, however, is meant to prepare us for the dramatic visions of the following Passus, where charity will be shown "in action". We are led thus to the next major stage of the Dreamer's progress, where moral growth and intellectual enlightenment culminate in the widening of vision. This is effected first by the re-entrance of Piers the Ploughman on the scene, secondly by the allegorical action centred on the Tree of Charity and, thereby, by the Dreamer's meeting with Faith in the person of Abraham (P. XVI), then with Hope (Moses), and Charity (the Christ-like figure of the Good Samaritan). They all endeavour to explain to Will the doctrine of the Trinity. But the last it is who, being the crowning element of the triad,[3] shows the most profound penetration of the Mystery, and can therefore reveal most fully in his inspired speech to the Dreamer how Love, springing from the very heart of the Godhead, manifested itself in the Incarnation and in the supreme act of Christ's sacrifice for mankind's Redemption (B, XVII). The next dream takes us to Jerusalem. We reach, thus, the climax of the whole poem with the narration of Christ's Passion and Harrowing of Hell, and His

3. Faith. Hope, and Charity are complementary to each other. But it is the third virtue that validates the other two, as Langland implies here through a re-enactment of the Gospel parable (XVII, 47-79) where the lovingkindness of the Samaritan shines once more to prove that "Fides sine operibus mortua est". Most of *Piers Plowman* could be labelled thus! This would be in point of fact another way to describe the theme of the poem.

victory over Sin and Death. The vision of Passus XVIII develops according to the liturgical sequence of Holy Week, and consists of a swift account of the Crucifixion, followed by a vivid description of the King of Glory storming Satan's kingdom against the background of suspense created by the debate between Mercy and Truth, Peace and Righteousness. The representation of these events, re-enacted before the enraptured Dreamer, not only provides the highest reach of poetic emotion in the entire poem, but reveals, as well, the focal centre of its inspiration and organization—the revelation, that is, of the ultimate, supreme truth that the Dreamer has been seeking for a long period of agonizing search. God's love, manifested in Christ's Death and Resurrection, is a token and a model for man that henceforth he must show boundless charity towards his fellow creatures. It is, as well, the indispensable means for his restoration to a full spiritual life. Announced by Holy Church in the Prologue, denied by men's cupidity, inquired into by Haukyn and Will, probed doctrinally by various allegorical characters throughout *Dowel* and *Dobet*,[4] Charity is the axis on which the whole conception turns. Through the knowledge and experience of this central virtue the Dreamer has come into contact with a divine reality in a kind of mystic trance, thereby gaining an insight into the timelessness of God's plan for mankind's salvation. The last lines of *Dobet* are a fitting conclusion to the *iter* of spiritual progress so far covered. From the contemplation of a supernatural vision, divinely bestowed, we return for a short while to real life. On waking the Dreamer rises for an act of thanksgiving and adoration with his wife and daughter, while the Easter Morning bells salute the Lord's and his own soul's resurrection. The homeliness of the tableau does not for a moment blur the ecstatic atmosphere established by the joyous hymns of *Te Deum laudamus* and *Ecce quam bonum* sung by the Four Daughters to celebrate the reconciliation of Justice and Love as well as the new peace between God and man:

4. See Patience's speech in XIII, 135-71; Anima's discourse on Charity, XV, 145-188; 204-262.

> Tyl the daye dawed this damaiseles daunced,
> That men rongen to the resurexioun and right with that I
>   waked,
> And called Kitte my wyf and Kalote my doughter—
> "Ariseth and reuerenceth goddes resurrexioun,
> And crepeth to the crosse on knees and kisseth it for a Iuwel!
> For goddess blissed body it bar for owre bote,
> And it afereth the fende for suche is the myghte,
> May no grysly gost glyde there it shadweth!"

(B, XVIII, 424-31)

> [Until the day dawned these damsels danced,
> When men rang bells for the Resurrection and straightaway I
>   woke.
> And I called Kit my wife and Kalote my daughter—
> "Rise up and honour God's resurrection,
> And creep to the cross on your knees and kiss it as a jewel!
> For it bore God's blessed body for our salvation,
> And such is its power that it frightens the Fiend,
> And no grisly spirit dare glide under its shadow."]

If we consider the main constitutive elements of the allegory in this second part of the *Vita* and its "denouement", we could easily feel inclined to establish a certain similarity of meaning and purpose with Dante's *Paradiso*. Undeniably, the entire third "cantica" is pervaded by an atmosphere of love, God's love, emotionally felt and doctrinally defined. One of the central themes here also is the mystery of the Incarnation, the Passion, and the triumph of Christ, discussed as truths and perceived as vision; while the presence of the Trinity hangs over the whole ascent of the Pilgrim and his Guide as a theological truth as well as a persistent musical motif. One might note, also, that just as happens in Passus XVI and XVII of the *Vita*, there occurs in the later cantos of Paradiso (XXIV-XXVI) a more effective understanding of, and a consequent growth in, Faith, Hope and Charity, as a preparatory step over the threshold into a closer vision of divine reality.[5] In general

5. A further striking analogy could be seen in the fact that, exactly as in Dobet, at various stages of the mystic ascent shining examples of virtue and

terms the progress portrayed in the visions of Dobet can be said
to parallel the constant upward course of *Paradiso,* in that it also
represents progress towards infinite Love and immutable Truth.
And, more important still, while these, in both poems, point
beyond the human, they are nevertheless the means by which God,
who draws human nature—as it were—towards the supernatural,
can thus transform it and make it divine. The differences, however,
are equally if not more evident than the similarities. Leaving aside
the actual narratives and the figurative elements together with the
allegorical frameworks which have nothing in common, and taking
into consideration only elements of thematic analogy, we can see
that the correspondence between them does not go very far.
Without going into details too much,[6] we may observe that in
Dante Love has a twofold connotation, a moral-spiritual one, and
one we might call philosophical. It is, first, the sublimation of the
natural impulses and desires from a finite to an infinite object,[7]
a sublimation totally realized in the transformation of the love
for a human being (Beatrice) into the love for the Divine Being.
Since God is the ultimate aspiration of the soul, it is only in the
identification of its will with the will of God that the perfection
of its joy and the fulfilment of its desire reside. This is what
Dante the Pilgrim learns from the blessed souls through Piccarda's
utterance which sums up the very essence and nature of Heaven:

holiness are shown in sharp contrast with instances of failure and neglect
on the part of those who, on earth, should uphold and practise them. Cf.
XI, 124-29; XII, 112-26; XXII, 70-93; XXI, 118-35. These passages refer,
all of them, to unworthy members of religious orders and prelates.

6. It would not be possible here to probe more extensively into possible
elements of contact between themes, doctrines, images and their poetical
expression by the two authors, although further investigation in this direction would, I believe, be rather rewarding and illuminating.

7. The nature of love and its operation in man's soul was discussed by
Virgil already in *Purg.,* XVII and XVIII, where it was analysed as the innate
force which bends man towards the object of his attraction, and therefore is
    ... sementa in voi d'ogni virtute
  e d'ogni operazion che merta pene.
                                              (XVII, 101-3)
    [... the seed in you of every virtue and
  of every action deserving punishment.]

Frate, la nostra volontà quieta
virtù di carità ...
                    (*Par.*, III, 70-1)
[Brother, the power of charity quiets our will ...]

And, in one of the most famous tercets of the poem:

E 'n la sua volontate è nostra pace:
ell'è quel mare al qual tutto si move
ciò ch'ella cria e che natura face.
                                    (ibid., 85-7)[8]
[And in his will is our peace: it is that sea
To which all things move, both what it creates
and what nature makes.]

And this is precisely what his spirit achieves through union with
the Godhead at the end of his journey, even though his soul is still
united with his body. Secondly, and intimately connected with the
elevation of the individual soul in one single and comprehensive
sweep, Love is perceived by the poet as the vital principle emanating from the Creator and keeping all that exists in perfect harmony, as the law that governs the universe and reduces all multiplicity to unity; in other words, a perception of love as a cosmic
force, consummated in the same final vision when Dante sees in
God "the mode or relationship which connects one thing with
another", all reality "as co-inhering in one simultaneous whole":[9]

Nel suo profondo vidi che s'interna,
legato con amore in un volume,
ciò che per l'universo si squaderna;
sustanze e accidenti e lor costume,

8. The same spirit and attitude of mind and heart seems to run through
Langland's lines: "Al was as thow wolde lorde, yworschiped be thow,/And
al worth as thow wolte what so we dispute!" (B, X, 127-8). ["All was as you
willed, o Lord, may you be praised,/And all will be as you wished no
matter what we say or think!"]
9. Sayers (and Reynolds), Transl. of *Par.* (1962), p. 18.

quasi conflati insieme, per tal modo
che ciò ch'i dico è un semplice lume.

(*Par.*, XXXIII, 85-90)

[In its depth I saw that it contained,
bound by love in one volume, that which
is scattered in leaves through the universe;
substances and accidents and their relations
as it were fused together in such a way that
what I tell of is a simple light.]

In Langland, on the other hand, the theme of love, central to, and,
as it were, constitutive in his poem—unmistakably the object of
as well as the answer to the search—is pursued in a simpler way
and, it must be added, more effectively in terms of practical Christianity. Defined earlier in Passus I as the essence of divine life and
the spring of its outward manifestation,[10] it could be recognized
also as the living spark implanted in man's heart:

And for to knowe it kyndly it comseth bi myght,
And in the herte, there is the heuede and the heigh welle;
For in kynde knowynge in herte there a myghte bigynneth.
And that falleth to the fader that formed vs alle, ...

(B, I, 161-4)

10. Cf. e.g.: And alle his werkes he wrougte with loue as him liste. (B, I,
147), [And He fashioned all his works, as he pleased, by the power of
love]; or:
For heuene myghte noughte holden it, it was so heuy of hymself,
Tyl it hadded of the erthe yeten his fylle,
And whan it haued of this folde flesshe and blode taken,
Was neuere leef vpon lynde lighter ther-after,
And portatyf and persant as the poynt of a nedle,
That myghte non armure it lette ne none heigh walles.

(ibid., 151-6)

[For Heaven could not hold love, it was so heavy in itself,
And it was not satisfied until it had eaten its fill of the earth,
And when it had taken on human flesh and blood,
It was lighter than a leaf on a linden tree ever was,
And as subtle and piercing as the point of a needle,
So that no armour or high walls could resist its power.]

[And in order to recognize it by natural instinct, it begins
        through some power
In the heart which is its source and well-spring;
For in the heart's instinctive knowledge there is a power
That comes from the Father who created us all, . . .]

A proposition, this, that echoes Dante's concept. But in the *Vita*
the idea evolves into the illustration of the evangelical command,
which is valid for all men, to love God and our neighbour. Total
abnegation and selflessness for the sake of our fellow creatures:
that is what Langland repeats simply and with increasing intensity.
As such love can be seen epitomized in Anima's words which
explain its meaning—a paraphrase almost of the Pauline text (Cor.
13, 1—1, 13).[11]

"Charitie", quod he, "ne chaffareth noughte ne chalengeth,
        ne craueth.
As proude of a peny as of a pounde of golde,
And is as gladde of a goune of a graye russet
As of a tunicle of Tarse or of trye scarlet.
He is gladde with alle gladde and good tyl alle wykked,
And leueth and loueth alle that owre lorde made.
Curseth he no creature ne he can bere no wratthe,
Ne no lykynge hath to lye ne laughe men to scorne.
Al that men seith, he let it soth and in solace taketh,
And alle manere meschiefs in myldenesse he suffreth;
Coueiteth he none erthly good but heuene-riche blisse."

(B, XV, 160-70)

["Charity", he said, "never bargains or challenges, or craves.
He is as proud of a penny as of a pound of gold,
And is as happy with a gown of grey wool
As with a tunic of Tartary silk or the finest scarlet.

11. St. Paul's teachings are central to Langland's inspiration, and bear on
his work as significantly as the Fathers or contemporary schoolmen. A closer
investigation of Paul's influence on Langland would help greatly, I feel, to
determine further the source of his thought.

He rejoices with those who rejoice and is good even to the
   wicked,
And trusts and loves all whom our Lord created.
He curses no creature nor can he bear any malice,
And he takes no delight in slandering or mocking others with
   scorn.
He gladly accepts as true all that men say,
And gently suffers all kinds of injuries;
He longs for no earthly good but only for the bliss of the
   kingdom of heaven."]

The quality of elemental tone and directness of diction, often
noted as characteristic of Langland's work, applies not only to
his style but, indeed, to the substance of his ideas. Obviously he is
concerned primarily with conveying truth for the benefit of a
popular audience,[12] so as to make of it the inspiration of their
daily life, in contrast with the more intellectually sophisticated
readers for whom Dante, seemingly, intended his Paradise.[13] A
down-to-earth, almost catechetical quality accompanies Langland's
verse in the majority of the visions related in *Dobet*—even the
most inspired and sublime—giving them, very often, a practical
purpose and a homiletic direction.[14] This fact, on the other hand,
does not diminish but rather enhances the dramatic action which
fills the narrative, and enlivens the allegorical meaning. Thus, for
instance, the encounter with Abraham, Moses and the Samaritan
not only signifies the Dreamer's growth in Faith, Hope and Charity
and the solution of apparent conflicts between the values of each
virtue, but is also the dramatic illustration of the biblical events
heralding the coming of Christ.[15] In *Paradiso*, on the contrary, the

12. This aspect of *Piers Plowman* has been illustrated extensively by
G. R. Owst, *Preaching in Medieval England,* Cambridge 1926, who defined
the poem "the quintessence of English medieval preaching" (p. 295). It is,
of course, much more than that.
   13. Cf. *Par.,* II, 1-6. "O voi che siete in picioletta barca . . ." etc.
   14. Cf. A. C. Spearing, "The Art of Preaching and *Piers Plowman*" in
Criticism and Medieval Poetry, London 1964, p. 73 ff.
   15. D. C. Fowler sees in these scenes elements derivative from the cycle
plays. He emphasises at the same time Langland's original adaptation of
traditional pageants. Cf. op. cit., pp. 128-9.

acquisition of the three virtues as the essential condition for God's revelation to the soul is expressed by means of a solemn examination by the three best qualified saints (Peter, James and John) and carried out in the intellectual atmosphere of a medieval classroom. Here the Pilgrim's answers, given in the most precise and orthodox terms, resolve themselves into the clearest, unswerving profession of what Dante

> ... ama bene e bene spera e crede.
>
> *(Par.,* **XXIV, 40)**

The strictly doctrinal quality of these cantos (XXIV-XXVI) does not involve cold didacticism; rather they are animated by resoundingly emotive poetry.[16] Similarly the omnipresent theme of the Trinity, which underlines for both poets the progressive increase of grace in the soul, is developed by Dante mainly as an ever-deepening intuition of the theological mystery, usually expressed in condensed, splendid "figurations" or definitions, like the following:

> Guardando nel suo Figlio con l'Amore
>   che l'uno e l'altro eternalmente spira,
>   lo primo e ineffabile Valore, ...
>
> *(Par.,* **X, 1-3)**
>
> [Looking on His Son with the love which the One
> and the Other eternally breathe forth, the primal
> and ineffable Power, ...]

or:

> O luce eterna che sola in te sidi,
>   sola t'intendi, e da te intelletta

---

16. As Momigliano notes in his commentary: "Sullo scheletro della scolastica passa l'onda d'una sonata d'organo ... Le somiglianze stilistiche fra quest'esame e le pagine di poesia didascalica sono superficiali" (op. cit., pp. 759, 761). ["A wave of organ music passes over the skeleton of Scholasticism ... the stylistic resemblances between this examination and the pages of didactic poetry are superficial."]

e intendente te ami e arridi!

(Par., XXXIII, 124-26)

[O Light Eternal, that alone abidest in Thyself,
alone knowest Thyself, and, known to Thyself
and knowing, lovest and smilest on Thyself!]

Langland, on the contrary, expatiates on it at length in the effort
not only to explain the doctrine in popular terms, but also to
emphasize its relevance for the daily life of men, and for their
spiritual elevation:

And to a torche or a tapre the Trinitee is lykened;
As wex and a weke were twyned togideres,
And thanne a fyre flaumende forth oute of bothe;
And as wex and weyke and hote fyre togyderes
Fostren forth a flaumbe and a feyre leye,
So doth the sire and the sone and also *spiritus sanctus*
Fostren forth amonges folke loue and bileue,
That alkyn Crystene clenseth of synnes.

(B, XVII, 203-10)[17]

[And the Trinity is compared to a torch or a taper;
Just as wax and wick are joined together,
So that a flame then flashes forth from both together;
And just as wax and wick and hot fire together
Foster flame and brilliant light,
So does the Father and the Son and the Holy Spirit
Kindle among the people love and faith,
That cleanse all kinds of Christians of their sins.]

Finally, with regard to the central Christ-theme, we may observe
that in Dante it occurs in a number of highly condensed visions,

17. This is just one example of the many illustrations of the Trinitarian
doctrine which runs throughout *Dobet* with unchanging tone of exposition,
but with a remarkable variety of images. See e.g. XVI, 181-224 (wedlock,
widowhood, virginity); XVII, 138-202 (fist, fingers, palm of the hand);
XVII, 244-59 (flint, tow, and spark). It is a skilful use of analogies by which
the poet applies the doctrine to men's life in order to stress particularly the
sins against the Holy Ghost.

where the Pilgrim beholds in momentary flashes the blinding radiance within which now the triumph of the Cross, now the fruits of the Redemption, or the mystery of Christ's "Humanity-Divinity" are glimpsed.[18] In Langland we have, instead, an extensive account of Christ's earthly career—elaborated over and over again—as the true embodiment of the ideals of Dowel, Dobet, and Dobest, and a powerful drama of Death and Life portraying the struggle of a valiant Knight who conquers the forces of darkness and quenches his thirst for men's souls.[19] In general terms, then, the *Dobet* section of the *Vita* can be viewed as corresponding to the third cantica of the *Commedia,* in that it contains a gradual revelation of divine Love to the soul, together with an increasing penetration of Truth. But the actual terms of visionary activity are different, as are, after all, the nature and finality of the mystic contemplation experienced by the Dreamer and the Pilgrim of *Paradiso.* As E. Salter puts it: "A direct vision of God the poem (*Piers Plowman*) certainly does not give us; it does give, however, in the Piers-Christ relationship, and in the endless drama of the Passion, Resurrection and Harrowing of Hell, an account of the nature and operation of the love which 'stands for vision', and an intimation of the divine source of that love".[20]

Perhaps if we take a glance again at the *Vita* with reference to the *Purgatorio* we may discover a greater possibility of establishing a certain degree of parallelism, especially if we include in our consideration the final stages of *Piers Plowman,* that is Passus XIX and XX which contain the *Dobest* section.

There are two important features, together with some concomitant aspects bearing significantly on the allegorical sequence, that prompt the attentive reader to recognize a striking measure of similarity between the two poems at this point of their structural development. In order to point out these correspondences it seems

---

18. Cf. *Par.,* XIV, 97-108. XXIII, passim; XXXIII, 127-32.
19. Christ's life and deeds are referred to in B, XVI, 90-166; Passus XVIII is, of course, wholly taken by this theme, which runs also well into Passus XIX (16-193).
20. Op. cit., p. 103.

to me opportune first to reconsider the central figure of Piers the Ploughman, and to try to enlarge our appreciation of his role and function in the B text of the *Vita*. In doing so a convincing parallel, I believe, can be found with the role and function of Beatrice in the *Commedia,* especially in the *Purgatorio.* No matter how markedly different the "origin" and actual connotation of the *persona* Piers, the essential meaning of the part played by him may, I suggest, be reduced to the same allegorical pattern as characterizes the figure of Beatrice. The transformation of Piers from the endearing ploughman of the *Visio,* model of simple virtue and guide to the good life, into the repository and authoritative expositor of truth in *Dobet* and *Dobest* may not be identical with the transfiguration of Dante's Lady, whose role as co-participant in his redemption is clearly established at the beginning of the *Commedia.*[21] Some important analogies must, however, be pointed out.

The second "epiphany" of Piers is prepared by means of references to him in the *Vita* which, on the one hand, foretell his deeper understanding of spiritual matters and, consequently, place him in a supernatural plane, and, on the other, are charged with a sense of emotional urgency and anxious expectation comparable to what we find in *Purgatorio* with regard to Beatrice. To Dante, who harbours some serious doubt about the efficacy of the penitents' prayers, Virgil replies:

> "Veramente a così also sospetto
>   non ti fermar se quella nol ti dice
>   che lume fia tra 'l vero e lo 'ntelletto.
> Non so se m'intendi; io dico di Beatrice:
>   tu la vedrai di sopra, in su la vetta
>   di questo monte, ridere e felice."
> E io: "Segnore, andiamo a maggior fretta,
>   ché già non m'affatico come dianzi,
>   e vedi omai che 'l poggio l'ombra getta."

(Purg., VI, 43-51)

---

21. *Inf.,* II, 52-120.

["Nevertheless, in so deep a question do not
take thy stand unless she tell thee of it who
shall be light between the truth and the intellect.
I know not if thou understandest, I speak
of Beatrice: thou shalt see her above
on the summit of this mountain, smiling
and in bliss."
And I said: "My Lord, let us make more haste,
for now I do not weary as before, and see how
the hill now casts its shadow."]

Again, when dealing with the nature of true love which the more
it increases the more there are to share in it, Beatrice is naturally
the one who will supply a complete and satisfying explanation:

"E se la mia ragion non ti disfama,
    vedrai Beatrice, ed ella pienamente
    ti torrà questa e ciascun'altra brama."

(Purg., **XV**, 76-8)

["And if my speech do not relieve thy hunger,
thou shalt see Beatrice and she will deliver
thee wholly from this and every other craving."]

Whenever a problem offers difficulties which go beyond the range
of human reason, the Pilgrim of Purgatory is referred to the one
who personifies supernatural truth.

Ed elli a me: "Quanto ragion qui vede
dir ti poss'io; da indi in là t'aspetta
pur a Beatrice, ch'é opera di fede."

(Purg., **XVIII**, 46-8)

[And he said to me: "As far as reason sees here
I can tell thee; beyond that wait only for Beatrice,
for it is matter of faith."]

It is not hard to detect in the mentions of Piers the same attitude of
trusting reliance for the solution of any major dilemma which the

Dreamer is faced with in his search. Following Clergye's own admission of the superiority of Love over all sciences, the words which contain the promise of Piers's coming re-echo, to some extent, the above references to Beatrice:

> "I can nought her-on." quod Conscience, "ac I knowe wel
>   Pieres;
> He wil nought agein holy writ speken I dar wel vndertake;
> Thanne passe we ouer til Piers come and preue this in dede."
> (B, XIII, 130-32)
> ["I cannot understand that," said Conscience, "but I know
>   Piers well;
> I can vouch for it that he will say nothing against holy writ;
> So let us leave this question until Piers comes to prove that in
>   practice."]

Later on, when Will acquires from Anima's discourse a deeper understanding of Charity and voices his eagerness to experience it even more closely, we are made aware of the indispensability of Piers if a fuller revelation of higher things is required:

> "By Cryst, I wolde that I knewe him," quod I, "no creature
>   leuere."
> "With-outen helpe of Piers Plowman," quod he, "his persone
>   seestow neuere."
> "Where clerkes knowen hym," quod I, "that kepen holy-
>   kirke?"
> "Clerkes haue no knowyng," quod he, "but by werkes and
>   bi wordes.
> Ac Piers the Plowman parceyueth more depper
> What is the wille and wherfore that many wyghte suffreth."
> There-fore by coloure ne by clergye knowe shaltow hym
>   neuere,
> Noyther thorw wordes ne werkes but thorw wille one.
> And that knoweth no clerke ne creature in erthe,
> But Piers the Plowman *Petrus, id est Christus.*
> (B, XV, 189-94; 203-6)

["By Christ, I would that I knew him," I said, "no other
creature more than him."

"Without the help of Piers Plowman," said he, "you will
never see him in person."

"Do the priests who rule holy church," I said, "know him?"

"Priests have no real knowledge of him," he said, "except
through works and words.

But Piers the Plowman sees more deeply

The purposes and causes for which many creatures suffer."

Therefore neither appearances nor learning will ever help you
to know him,

Neither will you recognize him merely in words or deeds but
by means of will alone.

And that neither scholar nor creature of this earth compre-
hends

Except Piers the Plowman—*Peter, that is Christ.*]

The progressive exaltation of Piers reaches here its highest point,
and this helps to explain that sense of urgent expectancy whose
momentum grows in the Dreamer until we come to the dramatic
climax (which precedes his entering a kind of inner dream), where
he swoons at the mere mention of Piers's name:

"Piers the Plowman!", quod I tho and all for pure ioye
That I herde nempne his name anone I swouned after ...

(B, XVI, 18-9)

["Piers the Plowman!", I exclaimed then and because of the
sheer joy I felt

On hearing his name mentioned I fell into a swoon straightaway.]

Likewise Dante was able to overcome the last obstacle on the way
of his arduous ascent when, trembling with emotion merely on

... udendo il nome
che ne la mente sempre mi rampolla

(*Purg.,* XXVII, 41-2)

> [... hearing the name
> that ever springs up in my mind]

he feels that the apparition of his Beloved is near at hand, "in tutta la sua travolgente vicina efficacia" ["in all the sweeping closeness of her power"].22

But, of course, it is at some significant moments of the subsequent visions that we can perceive a revealing measure of likeness between Beatrice and Piers, since it is there that the full impact of their bodily presence and the effect of their intervention in the action of both poems are felt more vigorously. In terms of moral structure it is interesting to note that the appearance of Piers occurs at what we may call an intermediate stage in the Dreamer's spiritual progress, between, that is, the period of moral education and intellectual instruction on one side, and direct revelation of divine truths on the other. Similarly, Dante's encounter with Beatrice takes place at the completion of his ascetical pilgrimage over the Mountain and marks his penetration into the supernatural atmosphere of the Earthly Paradise. This may be sufficient to justify our attempt to relate, however partially, the contents of the *Dobet* and *Dobest* Passus—in some significant aspects of their allegorical application—to those of the third part of the *Purgatorio*. The chief common pattern permitting such a comparison is the fact that the final act, so to speak, of the protagonists' spiritual renewal is performed within the framework of a biblical narrative where the drama of the Fall of Man, the Redemption, and the Apostolic Age unfolds itself continuously even down to the poets' time. Naturally there is a different use of traditional material made by each poet, together with a diverse positioning of or emphasis on events. Thus, at the beginning of Passus XVI, on swooning for joy at Anima's mention of Piers, the Dreamer falls into a deeper dream to behold the return of the good Ploughman:

22. Ulrich Leo, "Il Canto XXVII del Purgatorio" in *Letture Dantesche* (a cura di G. Getto), Firenze 1963, p. 1219.

> And laye longe in a lone dreme and atte laste me thoughte
> That Pieres Plowman al the place me shewed,
> And bad me toten on the tree on toppe and on rote.
> With thre pyles was it vnder-pighte I perceyued it sone.
>
> (lines 20-23)
>
> [And I lay for a long time in a lonely dream and eventually
>   it seemed to me
> That Piers Plowman appeared there to show me the whole
>   place,
> And bade me to gaze at the tree from its top to its roots.
> Soon I saw that it was supported by three props.]

We have reached the heights, and we may assume this place to be
the Garden of Eden, and the tree to be the biblical plant of
knowledge of good and evil.[23] But we are not allowed to stop at
this suggestion for, according to Anima's indications immediately
preceding the above lines, the garden is man's heart and the tree
growing in it is the Tree of Charity, with Free Will farming the
land as a sub-tenant of Piers Plowman (ibid., 4-17). The three
props supporting the tree—Piers soon explains to the Dreamer—
are the Persons of the Trinity, and are meant to defend it from the
World, the Flesh, and the Devil. Here follows one of the most
elaborate allegories of the poem with the tree blossoming out into
several strange "ramifications" and complex transformations. In
Piers's words it becomes in stages a symbol of the Trinity itself
and of mankind, while its branches bear the fruits of Marriage,
Continence and Virginity. These fruits, soon afterwards, become
Adam, Abraham, Isaiah, and John the Baptist; and when Piers, at
the Dreamer's request, shakes them down the Devil carries them
away into Hell, pursued by Piers who seizes the second stake,
Filius, thus precipitating the Incarnation (ibid., 24-89). Whatever
the difficulties in interpreting the vision—and they are consider-

___

23. Cf. D. C. Fowler, op. cit., p. 119-20. Soon afterwards, however, this
critic remarks: "This is not, of course, the literal tree we find in the Garden
of Eden. The poet assumes that we have the literal tree in mind (as we do
once we are aware of the poem's biblical structure), and goes on, appropriately, to let Soul describe it tropologically" (p. 121). See also the important notes on the scene on p. 227.

able[24]—the important thing to note is that Piers here appears to the Dreamer as a semi-divine person, mysteriously assumed into a supernatural world of grace, in intimate contact with God's realities and partaking of His truths. He can therefore introduce Will the Dreamer to the contemplation of events concerning Man's destiny, from his creation in God's image to his fall at the hands of the lurking Enemy, and on to the promise of his regeneration by the Son's atonement. It is a representation, in terms of expository allegory as well as of allegory of action, of the pre-Christian era and, at the same time, an insight into the working of God in human history. It is, moreover, a representation in which Piers acts as an authoritative interpreter of eternal truths as well as a determining agent of the process whereby the tree of mankind, stripped bare of its fruits of love, can again flourish in full

24. Most commentators of *Piers Plowman* confess at this point their bewilderment and perhaps one has to be content with an interpretation in general terms of the overall meaning of the passage. Professor Donaldson, for instance, in his detailed discussion of the scene (op. cit., pp. 183-92), feels that Piers "remains ambiguous and even redundant" since his function could lend itself to several simultaneous identifications: mankind, the prophets, Christ, God the Father. It is hard not to share this critic's conclusion: "Twentieth-century inability to comprehend fourteenth-century allegory possibly accounts for some of our bewilderment, but one wonders whether it was not shared by a good many unsubtle, literal-minded medieval readers —whether, indeed, the incident of the Tree of Charity as it dictated itself to the B-author in terms of poetry is altogether susceptible of satisfactory rational explanation. The allegory seems too complex, too crowded" (p. 187). All that argues convincingly of course for the complete elimination of Piers and his being replaced by Liberum Arbitrium by the C-poet. See also R. W. Frank, op. cit., pp. 86-7. On the other hand E. Salter while admitting that "if we try to trace exact continuity in the allegorical pattern, we shall find discrepancies", attempts to explain the scene in terms of stylistic appreciation and concludes that "fluctuation of allegorical depth is a feature of the whole poem, but is seen here in a particularly dramatic form" (op. cit., pp. 75-6). She does not, however, give a satisfactory interpretation of the meaning of the passage. Finally, one could hardly reject Mr. Fowler's opinion that Langland's "account of the Fall of Man is ... a remarkable example of simultaneous dramatization on the four levels of meaning in scriptural tradition" (op. cit., p. 121). But it is not easy to accept his suggestion that in order to make the scene perfectly clear we should avoid fitting Piers "into the allegorical action", and only consider him as a "director" of it (cf. pp. 119-128). This would diminish somehow, I think, the importance Langland wanted to give the central figure of his poem.

blossom of "Reuthe", "Boxome-Speche", "Benygne-Lokynge", and "Lele-Wordes, the lawe of Holycherche": these all grow into the "frute Charite" (XVI, 1-9).

Piers's entrance on the scene is not as solemn and triumphant as Beatrice's,[25] just as the presentation of Piers's "gardyne", barely hinted at in the poem, and invested straightaway with a tangle of allegorical details, has very little to do with the lengthy description of the "divina foresta spessa e viva" (*Purg.*, XXVIII, 1-33) of Dante's Earthly Paradise. There the landscape element is allowed major pictorial scope, although its symbolic character remains perfectly clear. Yet what we see happening in Piers's garden is highly reminiscent of one of the central episodes in the sacred pageant witnessed by the Pilgrim at the summit of the Mountain. In the middle of the mystical procession, in fact, there also stands the Tree of Human Kind:

> Io senti' mormorare a tutti: "Adamo!";
> poi cerchiaro una pianta dispogliata
>   di fiori e d'altra fronda in ciascun ramo.
>
> (Purg., XXXII, 37-9)
>
> [I heard a murmur from them all of "Adam!"
> Then they encircled a tree stripped of its flowers
> and all its foliage in every branch.]

The higher it rises the wider it spreads so as to reveal the purpose of God's creation of Mankind who was destined in its totality for Heaven, while its bareness bespeaks Adam's fallen nature, and the tragic reality of sin. Only when the Gryphon-Christ in his unfallen nature and humanity binds the Chariot-pole to the Tree does it break into blossom, acquiring the new life which the power of the Cross and the legacy of Christ's Church bring into the world. And we must not forget that Beatrice is there too, almost at the centre of the scene, taking part, like Piers, in the events that repeat the story of Man both eternal and temporal, and show his relationship with God. Although she does not "direct" the action like Piers, her appearance on the Gryphon-driven cart— which symbolizes the Church (canto XXX)—and her remaining

25. See above, p. 133 ff.

beneath the Tree to guard it after Christ and his company have
risen to Heaven show her to be the incarnation of revealed Truth
or the earthly image of Divine Wisdom. This matches one of the
possible interpretations of Piers's role in the vision just discussed,
even though the latter cannot obviously be said to correspond in
all its details to the former.[26] Together, however, the two visions
contain one important aspect which associates them in a single
common perspective, if viewed from the standpoint of both the
Pilgrim's and Dreamer's spiritual advancement. And that is the
fact that their reaching from a human to a divine plane of reality
coincides with the enlargement of their personal progress into the
visualization of the problem of salvation for all mankind, the
insertion, that is, of an individual experience into a universal one.
It is an eloquent mark both of Dante's and of Langland's Christianity that they think of the things of Faith in terms of eschatology,
for both share a deep consciousness of the common destiny of men
heading for the same goal on the way fixed by God. Such an attitude is, of course, present throughout the poems, but here it
acquires a particular relevance. Moreover, since the presence of
Beatrice and Piers constitutes a determining factor in these revelations, it follows almost as a corollary that their illuminative function goes beyond the task of helping to solve the problem of
salvation for one single individual, and reaches out to the wider
dimensions of an enormous spiritual force valid for the elevation
of the whole human race. Perhaps there is no more eloquent
example of these two figures possessing such singular power than
what appears to be the climatic moment of the regenerative experience of both Dante and Will—the encounter of their souls with
Christ. The "figuration" of this event, admittedly, is realized in
the two poems by means of dissimilar images, which do not, however, obliterate the basic similarity. The fulcrum of the whole
representation is, in both texts, the coming into communion with
the Incarnate Deity (Jesus) after the hard-won renewal through
penance, felt and visualized through an intense liturgical move-

26. Cf. Donaldson, op. cit., p. 184. footnote 4, where he quotes Miss Day
(*RES*, III, 334) who proposed such an interpretation. Professor Donaldson
does not accept entirely this suggestion.

ment in the midst of which the persons of Beatrice as well as of Piers stand in such a prominent position as to become the very agents of this communion. We saw already how the glorified Lady fulfils such a sacramental function within the splendours of the mystic pageant. Borne on the Chariot of the Church she appears as the "presentation" of the Eucharist since—we may add now— the whole picture is suggestive of the veiled monstrance of the Host borne in a *Corpus Christi* procession. Besides, the singing of *Benedictus qui venis*—a manifest adaptation of the hymn chanted in the Mass before the consecration and referring properly to Christ (Matt. XXI, 9; John XII, 13)), but here introducing Beatrice—makes unmistakably clear the poet's symbolic intention. And it is not surprising therefore to see the Pilgrim subsequently gazing into her eyes and seeing in them the reflection of Christ's light shining with his human and divine natures. Beatrice's intermediary and revelatory function could not be more deeply conceived. Now, Langland's intuition of the Ploughman's parallel role in relation to the Dreamer is developed, I would suggest, on practically the same lines; but it is presented in a more dramatic fashion which, in comparison, makes Dante's "figure" seem rather static for all its solemnity. Piers's intimate connection with Christ, in fact, is shown within the full-blooded narrative of the Passion, the Harrowing of Hell, and the Resurrection, which the poet draws from the Gospel story and enlivens with the romance motif of a joust. In this scene also, set in the Jerusalem of Palm Sunday, there resounds the joyous cry hailing Christ's coming, but in the semblance of Piers the Ploughman:

> *Benedictus qui venit in nomine Domini.*
> Thanne I frayned at Faith what al that fare be-mente,
> And who sholde iouste in Iherusalem. "Iesus", he seyde,
> "And fecche that the fende claymeth Piers fruit the Plowman."
> "Is Piers in this place?" quod I, and he preynte on me,
> "This Iesus of his gentrice wole Iuste in Piers armes,
> In his helme and in his haberioun *humana natura;*
> That Cryst be nought biknowe here for *consummatus deus,*
> In Piers paltok the Plowman this priker shal ryde;

For no dynte shal hym dere as *in deitate patris.*"

(B, XVIII, 18-26)

[*Blessed is he that cometh in the name of the Lord.*
Then I asked Faith what all that business meant,
And who was to joust in Jerusalem. "Jesus," he said,
"To win back what the Fiend claims—Piers Plowman's fruit."
"Is Piers in this place?" said I, and he gazed firmly at me,
"This Jesus because of his chivalrous nobility will joust in
    Piers's coat of arms,
And in his helmet and coat of mail, *human nature;*
So that He may be not recognized here as *Almighty God,*
In Piers Plowman's apparel shall this knight ride:
For no blow shall harm Him as He is the Son of his divine
    Father."]

The same vividness of imagery presides over the next vision at
the beginning of *Dobest,* intensifying the emotional strain felt by
the Dreamer, who during Mass on Easter morning contemplates,
as it were, the substance of Christ's sacrifice symbolized in the
sacrament of the Eucharist:

In myddes of the masse tho men yede to offrynge,
I fel eftsones a-slepe and sodeynly me mette,
That Piers the Plowman was paynted al blody,
And come in with a crosse bifor the comune peple,
And righte lyke in alle lymes to owre lorde Iesu;
And thanne called I Conscience to kenne me the sothe.
"Is this Iesus the Iuster?" quod I, "that Iuwes did to deth?
Or it is Pieres the Plowman? who paynted hym so rede?"
Quod Conscience, and kneled tho "thise aren Pieres armes,
His coloures and his cote-armure ac he that cometh so blody
Is Cryst with his crosse conqueroure of Crystene."

(B, XIX, 4-14)

[In the middle of Mass when the people went to make their
    offerings,
I fell asleep again and suddenly I dreamt
That I saw Piers the Plowman all stained with blood

> Come in with a cross before the people,
> Looking in all his limbs exactly like our Lord Jesus;
> Then I called out to Conscience to tell me the truth.
> "Is this Jesus the Jouster?" I said, "whom the Jews put to death?
> Or is it Piers the Plowman? Who painted him so red?"
> Conscience spoke as he kneeled down then: "These are Piers's arms,
> His colours and his armour, but he that comes in so bloody
> Is Christ with his cross, the Conqueror of Christians."]

Now one may well ask: do these passages suggest a complete identification of Piers with Christ? On the face of it the lines seem to warrant such a conclusion, especially if viewed in the light of the previous reference to the Ploughman *Petrus, id est Christus* (B, XV, 206). But I do not think Langland intended to make of Piers another God, and if he ever comes near the doctrine or the idea of deification both here and in the episode of the Tree of Chairty,[27] he does so in the perfectly orthodox sense that any human being who pursues the ideal of holiness and attains, through grace, a state of spiritual perfection, realizes the full potentiality of the divine spark implanted in him by God, and can, in some sense, make himself divine. He can therefore be looked upon as partaking intimately of God's life and possessing His attributes of Truth and Love. In this new identity a sanctified human person becomes best qualified to reveal them, and to mediate for those

27. We are reminded of the words spoken by Holy Church much earlier in the poem, following her statement about truth as the best of treasures:
> Who-so is trewe of his tonge and telleth none other,
> And doth the werkis ther-with and wilneth no man ille,
> He is a god bi the gospel agrounde and aloft,
> And ylike to owre lorde bi seynte Lukes wordes.

(B, I, 88-91)

> [Whoso is truthful in his speech and tells no lies,
> And acts in conformity with it and wishes ill to no man,
> Is a god, according to the Gospel, on earth and in heaven,
> And alike to our Lord, as St. Luke teaches.]

See in this connection the commentary of Robertson and Huppé, op. cit., p. 43. For an exhaustive discussion of the whole question cf. Donaldson, op. cit., pp. 186-7.

who seek the same ideal. We must assume that such is the case with Piers, and, in this respect, his role parallels that of Beatrice. Naturally Dante's exaltation of the latter can more easily be accepted, because the poet firmly believed her to be already a blessed soul enjoying God's vision. On this ground he could, understandably, make her his personal saint and guide.[28] On this understanding any further idealization must be based. And although Piers remains firmly grounded in this world as the ideal representative of the good life, he has grown so much in the possession of grace, so closely associated with divinity, as to become the Christlike figure *par excellence*. His transference into a supernatural state can be assumed not only in imaginative but in theological terms as well. He can be said, therefore, "to show us all the place" (B, XVI, 21)), or to be able to perceive "plenere tyme" (ibid., 103) and, in an apparently more daring transfiguration, reflect in himself, like Beatrice, the human and divine nature of Christ. In other words Piers is to the Dreamer the "God-bearing image", the figure who offers a vicarious knowledge of Christ, just as the Pilgrim of Purgatory came to encounter the Saviour *in* or *through* the person of Beatrice. In taking up a human being and endowing him with a function of the highest import, Langland was indeed in good company! In this respect it is no exaggeration to suggest that the central intuition of the special Christ-Piers relationship corresponds in a remarkable way to the Christ-Beatrice one, and thus offers a parallel to Dante almost without equal in the allegorical literature of the Middle Ages.

This correspondence, moreover, can be extended further to include another important aspect of the role played by Piers, which derives or, better, grows out of the above intuition. I refer to his next, and last, appearance in *Dobest*, which affords to the Dreamer the vision of the completion of God's scheme for the salvation of mankind.

28. See the excellent and illuminative essay on Beatrice by E. Gilson in his volume *Dante the Philosopher* (Transl. by David Moore), London 1948, pp. 72-82 and passim. Professor Gilson deals in this book mainly with philosophical problems in the *Convivio* and the *Monarchia*. But where he touches on the *Comedy* his approach is refreshing, and stimulating.

Passus XIX had opened with the Dreamer's participating in the Easter rite, and enjoying the fruits of the Redemption in the Sacrifice of the Mass. The vision now is enlarged to reveal the application of the same fruits of Christ's victory to the world, through the founding of the Church, his kingdom on earth. After a discussion by Conscience (who appears anew to assist Will, about to return to the world of actuality) on the meaning of the name "Christ", the Dreamer learns that he implemented Dowel and Dobet by his activity as teacher and healer. But Christ did "best" when, before the Ascension, he bestowed his legacy on Piers and his disciples, thus instituting the apostolic tradition. The Ploughman here becomes Christ's vicar on earth, wielding his authority and the power to dispense his pardon to those who fulfil the necessary conditions:

> And whan this dede was done Dobest he taughte,
> And gaf Piers power and pardoun he graunted
> To alle manere men mercy and forgyfnes,
> Hym myghte men to assoille of alle manere synnes
> In couenant that thei come and knowleche to paye,
> To Pieres pardon the Plowman *redde quod debes*.
>
> (B, XIX, 177-82)

> [And when this deed was done he taught Do-best,
> And gave Piers power, and granted him authority
> To dispense mercy and forgiveness to all men,
> And power to absolve them of all kinds of sins,
> On condition that they come and agree to pay restitution
> According to Piers the Plowman's pardon: *Pay that which thou owest.*]

Subsequently the Dreamer witnesses the descent of the Holy Ghost and the establishment of the visible Church. The main character appears to be *Grace*, "Crystes messager", who distributes the gifts of the Paraclete necessary for the new Society of the Faithful. But Piers is present too, sharing in the task of building the edifice of Christendom under the direction, and with the assistance of Grace, whose appointed representative, "procuratour and reve", he now

becomes.[29] Clearly the Ploughman here has come to represent
Peter, the head of the Church, and by extension the sacramental
office of the priesthood. In this regard the role of Piers can be
said to parallel that assumed by Beatrice in the sacred pageant on
the summit of Purgatory where, as we saw, she exercised also the
office of Christ's ministry in relation to the repentant Pilgrim. It
might be objected here that Langland's evident identification of
Piers with the "historical" St. Peter (the first High Priest of the
Church)—an identification perhaps made easier by the equivalence
of the name Piers and Peter—does not allow such a comparison,
since Beatrice's sacerdotal function is admittedly unfolded in the
context of Dante's personal confession. But just as the experience
of the *Commedia's* protagonist has an avowed typological value—
his, especially here, is the story of all men assumed into the stream
of the universal Church—so Beatrice's sacramental dignity goes
beyond the limits of one individual's redemption, and possesses a
wider symbolical reference. Besides the "significations" we have
noted already, this can be seen, for example, from the episode
recalled earlier where she appeared alone by the Tree of Christendom, to guard the Church:

> Sola sedeasi in su la terra vera
>   come guardia lasciata lì del plaustro
>   che legar vidi a la biforme fera.
> In cerchio le facevan di sé claustro
>   le sette ninfe, con quei lumi in mano
>   che son sicuri d'Aquilone e d'Austro.

(Purg., XXXII, 94-99)

> [She sat alone on the bare ground,
> left there as guardian of the chariot
> I had seen the bi-formed beast make fast.

---

29. J. F. Adams's suggestion in this respect is worth noting: "It is not
to be said that he (Piers) is Grace, nor that he symbolizes it, but rather that
he helps to understand it. If Piers himself is consistently to be understood as
anything specifically, it is as the arbiter between man and the proper understanding of Grace" (*"Piers Plowman* and the Three Ages of Man" in
J.E.G.Ph., lxi, 41).

> The seven nymphs in a ring made of themselves a
> cloister for her, with those lights in their hands
> which are safe from north wind and south.]

A few lines before these Christ was said to have risen to Heaven. Sitting "on the bare ground", surrounded by the Seven Virtues (cardinal and theological in association with the gifts of the Holy Spirit), Beatrice is not only an earthly image of Divine Wisdom, but clearly appears as the authoritative substitute for Christ, the Keeper of his Truth bequeathed to the world, and the priestly office entrusted to the apostles. In other words she represents, allegorically, the ideal *Sacerdotium* of the Church, uncorrupted in time.[30] Correspondingly, Piers besides symbolizing the Priestly Institution embodies, as well, the perpetuation of the primitive apostolic spirit in all its purity and efficacy throughout the ages. This can be inferred from the extensive account of his labours in setting up the barn of Unity, "holicherche on Englisshe", and subsequently when, on completion of his task, the scene shifts from the beginnings of Christianity to its conditions during the poet's own day. Of course one cannot go much further than to point to the basic similarity of a concept. Dante has enshrined it in the richly meaningful but static posture of Beatrice, whereas Langland elaborates it through the prolonged description of Piers's activity in building up the structure of the Church. The extended metaphor of ploughing, sowing and harvesting, in perfect keeping with the original connotation of the Ploughman in the poem, makes up in fact a picture concrete and dynamic at the same time. This, incidentally, stands in sharp contrast with the presentation of the Church structure as visualized in the opening procession of Dante's Earthly Paradise. What was there seen as a

---

30. Most commentators agree in this interpretation. Cf. e.g. L. Pietro-bono, *La Div. Com. di D.A.*, Firenze 1956, p. 438 ff. It is interesting to quote in this connection D. L. Sayers's remark: "It must be remembered that for Dante (as he says very plainly in *Par.*, XXVIII, 22-4), the Chair of Peter was 'vacant in the sight of the Son of God', because of the usurpation of Boniface VIII and the corruption of his successors. Moreover, at the time when he was writing the *Purgatorio*, the Popes had actually left Rome for Avignon; so that the See was 'vacant' in a double sense" (op. cit., p. 329).

grand spectacle where, in a perfectly schematic order, the personifications of the Books of the Old and New Testament, the Theological and Cardinal Virtues, the Acts and the Book of Revelation, the Epistles, advance slowly with the chariot of the Church, becomes, in the different rural imagery of *Piers Plowman*, a scene of intense action, in which practically the same scriptural personifications are shown to be engaged in forging the God-ordered organization of Christianity. Prominent among these are, in both poems, the four cardinal virtues, considered by the two poets here and elsewhere to be essential for the renovation of mankind. When Dante, in this context, makes them sing:

> "Noi siam qui ninfe e nel ciel siamo stelle:
> pria che Beatrice discendesse al mondo,
> fummo ordinate a lei per sue ancelle.
> Merrenti a li occhi suoi; ma nel giocondo
> lume ch'è dentro aguzzeranno i tuoi
> le tre di là, che miran più profondo."

(Purg., **XXXI**, 106-11)

> ["Here we are nymphs and in heaven are stars.
> Before Beatrice descended to the world we were
> ordained to be her handmaids. We will bring thee
> to her eyes; but for the happy light that is
> within them the three on the other side, who
> look deeper, shall quicken thine."]

we are given to understand that, besides being complementary to the theological ones, the natural virtues, given to men even before the Incarnation, have been fully restored by Christ, and as Beatrice's *handmaids* are destined to assist men in the perception of Revealed Truth and in their availing of the new life of grace which she symbolizes. They are, thus, instrumental for the achievement of perfection. It is an important, far-reaching doctrine which undoubtedly Langland shares. But whereas in Dante it remains a mere statement, in Langland its potentiality is handled in a more dynamic fashion in accordance with his more practical approach. For him also the cardinal virtues are closely connected with grace;

but they "are of crucial importance because the ordering of society depends upon their practice",[31] and in the hands of Piers they can help men to grow in love and truth:

> And Grace gaue greynes the cardynales vertues,[32]
> And sewe hem in mannes soule and sithen he tolde her names.
>
> (B, XIX, 269-70)
>
> [And Grace gave (to Piers) seeds of corn—the cardinal
>   virtues—
> To sow them in the souls of men, and afterwards explained
>   their names.]

How each of them works in the hearts of men is shown by the detailed analysis of their power and how each should be used in everyday life. And the conclusion is a further stressing of their practical function:

> Thise foure sedes Pieres sewe and sitthe he did hem harwe
> With olde lawe and newe lawe that loue myghte wexe
> Amonge the foure vertues and vices destroye.
>
> (ibid., 306-8)
>
> [These four seeds Piers sowed and afterwards he harrowed
>   them
> With the Old Law and the New Law, so that Love might grow
> Among the four virtues and destroy the vices.]

Thus ends Langland's sketch of the history of the Church given in a less splendid symbolic presentation than Dante's, but animated on the whole by a more realistic attitude and an active impulse which is, in the end, more accessible to the reader, as appears in the final image of this section:

31. J. F. Goodridge, op. cit., p. 49. Cf. also R. W. Frank, op cit., pp. 103-4. It must be remembered that Dante too is perfectly conscious of the importance of the cardinal virtues for an orderly development of man and society, morally and spiritually. He has stated this at the beginning of *Purgatorio* (I, 23); see also above, pp. 76-7.
32. The corresponding line in C has 'gaf to Peers'.

And whan this dede was done, Grace deuised
A carte, hyghte Cristendome, to carye Pieres sheues;
And gaf hym caples to his carte, Contricioun and Confes-
    sioun,
And made Presthode haywarde, the while hym-self went
As wide the worlde is with Piers to tulye treuthe.

(B, XIX, 326-30)

[And when this deed was accomplished, Grace constructed
A cart called Christendom to carry Piers's sheaves;
And gave him horses for his cart—Contrition and Confession—
And appointed Priesthood as a hayward, and then he himself
    went off
With Piers far and wide through the world in order to till
    Truth.

The correspondences (and differences) we have noted so far present
a further, even more striking, point of convergence in the closing
scenes of the *Purgatorio* and *Piers Plowman*. No one, in fact,
could fail to be impressed by the fact that in both poems the vision
of the Redemption and of the ideal Church, concomitant with the
attainment of individual renewal and the promise of universal
salvation, breaks, almost abruptly, to give place to a picture of
general corruption, violence and stupidity, revealing how far the
world of actuality is from implementing the programme of Christian activity just envisioned. The tragic pantomime witnessed by the
Pilgrim of the *Commedia* in the second part of the "Masque" in
the Garden of Eden has its counterpart in the swift drama watched
by the Dreamer in the last book of *Piers Plowman*. In both the
main feature is the coming of Antichrist to work havoc in a
divided Christendom and his apparent success, for a while, in
thwarting God's plan principally by means of the most universal
and only too common of human vices: cupidity. It is, however,
mainly in the way of structural coincidence that the similarity of
these scenes exists. For, although in many respects Langland's
picture of the Church's reversal echoes that of Dante, the general
perspective in which it is viewed, and the former's actual attitude, make it somehow different. The attack of the forces of evil is

seen by Dante in historical terms and visualized through a solemn scenography of apocalyptic proportions. It is a startling succession of the fateful events that came very near to undoing the Church in the course of centuries: the persecutions of Imperial Rome, the heresies and schisms, the corrupting gift of Constantine, the meretricious relationship of the Papacy with the House of France and the consequent betrayal of Christian Rome. None of these events is explicitly mentioned. Each, instead, is represented either by the virulent onslaught of nightmarish beasts, like the eagle and the fox plunging on the cart and shattering it,[33] or the apparition of a dragon issuing from the gaping earth and tearing off portion of it; and lastly, most terribly, by the monstrous metamorphoses in which the poet's use of the Apocalypse appears most directly:

33. *Purg.*, XXXII, 109-35. In this canto the Donation of Constantine (referred to also in 136-41) is figured in the following passage:

> Poscia per indi ond'era pria venuta,
>   l'aguglia vidi scender giù ne l'arca
>   del carro e lasciar lei di sé pennuta:
> E qual esce di cuor che si rammarca,
>   tal voce uscì del cielo e cotal disse:
>   "O navicella mia, com mal se' carca!"

(lines 124-9)

[Then, from the place it came from before, I saw the eagle descend into the body of the car and leave it feathered with its plumage; and such a voice as comes from a grieving heart I heard come forth from heaven and it said: "O my little bark, with how much ill art thou laden!"]

What Dante here says by means of a symbolic image, Langland describes plainly, but with equal effectiveness, in a passage contained in Anima's speech:

> Whan Costantyn of curteysye holykirke dowed
> With londes and ledes lordeshipes and rentes,
> An angel men herde an heigh at Rome crye,
> "*Dos ecclesie* this day hath ydronke venym,
> And tho that han Petres powere arn apoysoned alle."

(B, XV, 519-23)

[When Constantine out of generosity endowed the Church
With lands and subjects, estates and rents,
Men heard an angel cry high above Rome,
"This day the true wealth of the Church has drunk venom,
And those who have Peter's power are all poisoned."]

Both poets, of course, make use here of a widely current story often referred to by moralists and reformers in the Middle Ages.

Quel che rimase, come da gramigna
   vivace terra, de la piuma, offerta
   forse con intenzion sana e benigna,
sì ricoperse, e funne ricoperta
   e l'una e l'altra rota e 'l temo, in tanto
   che più tiene un sospir la bocca aperta.
Trasformato così 'l dificio santo
   mise fuor teste per le parti sue,
   tre sovra 'l temo e una in ciascun canto.
Le prime eran cornute come bue,
   ma le quattro un sol corno avean per fronte:
   simile mostro visto ancor non fue.
Sicura quasi rocca in alto monte
   seder sov'esso una puttana sciolta
   m'apparve con le ciglia intorno pronte;
e, come per che non li fosse tolta,
vidi di costa a lei dritto un gigante;
   e baciavansi insieme alcuna volta.

(Purg., XXXII, 136-53)[34]

[What was left was covered again, as fertile soil with dog-grass, with the plumage, offered perhaps with pure and gracious intent, and the one and the other wheel and the shaft were covered with it in less time that a sigh keeps open the lips.

Thus transformed, the holy structure put forth heads on its parts, three on the shaft and one at each corner, the three horned like oxen and the four with a single horn on the fore-head; such a monster was never seen.

Secure, like a fortress on a high mountain, appeared to me an ungirt harlot seated on it, looking about her with bold brows, and as if that she might not be taken from him I saw a giant standing beside her, and they kissed each other again and again.]

The episode ends with the giant scourging the harlot and bearing the car into the depths of the forest (a clear indication of the transference of the Papal See to Avignon). It is a "wonderfully

---

34. Cf. *Rev.*, XII, 3-4; XVII, 3; XVIII, 3.

virulent bad dream"[35] that desecrates the Garden of Eden and leaves it empty.

Langland's vision of the Church's overthrow is not so compact and dense an allegory, nor so solemn and awe-inspiring in the plastic movements of its actors. It is instead a magnificent combination of the grim and farcical, opening out into a riotous mêlée where the external confusion of the forces battling around the "Castle of Unity" matches the internal confusion of the feckless humanity that has failed to understand and cherish properly God's will as manifested in Christ. Undeniably there are moments of apocalyptic grandeur, as, for example, that which opens the Dreamer's last vision of Antichrist who comes, not in the guise of symbolic animals as in Dante, but in his own terrifying self:

> in mannes forme,
> Antecryst cam thanne and al the croppe of treuthe
> Torned it vp so doune and ouertilte the rote,
> And made fals sprynge and sprede and spede mennes nedes;
> In eche a contre there he cam he cutte awey treuthe,
> And gert gyle growe there as he a god were.

> (B, XX, 51-6)

> [in human form
> Antichrist then came and turned upside down all the tree of Truth
> So that the root was above the crown,
> And caused falsehood to grow and spread and increase men's hunger for riches;
> In every country into which he came he uprooted Truth,
> And made guile grow as though he were a god.]

A second instance occurs shortly afterwards, when the poet seems to take relish in describing minutely the loathsome diseases which Nature sends down from the planets upon the army of the fiend and all those who have succumbed to his attack and joined him, while Conscience and other "fools" remain defensively inside "Unity" (ibid., 79-86). The clear reference to the Black Death

35. F. Ferguson, *Dante*, London 1963, p. 162.

becomes more pointed in the following lines where the inspiration from the *Book of Revelation* is accompanied by a certain amount of grim humour:

> Elde the hore he was in the vauntwarde,
> And bare the banere bifor Deth by righte he it claymed.
> . . . .
> So Kynde thorw corupciouns kulled ful manye.
> Deth cam dryuende after and al to doust passhed
> Kynges and knyghtes kayseres and popes;
> Lered ne lewed he let no man stonde,
> That he hitte euene that euere stired after.
> Many a louely lady and lemmanes of knyghtes
> Swouned and swelted for sorwe of Dethes dyntes.
>
> (B, XX, 94-5; 98-104)
>
> [Hoary Old Age was in the vanguard,
> And bore the banner before Death, a position which he
>   claimed as by his right.
> . . . .
> So Nature with cruel diseases killed a great many.
> Death came dashing after him and crushed all to dust,
> Kings and knights, emperors and popes;
> He left no one standing, neither learned nor ignorant.
> Those he hit squarely never stirred afterwards.
> Many a lovely lady and the mistresses of knights
> Swooned and died in the pain of Death's blows.]

The Deadly Sins are not absent here. But they do not impress us so much as being "seuene grete gyauntz,/That with Antecrist helden" (lines 214-15) but rather as conspicuous personifications of vice, portrayed with more dramatic repulsiveness even than in the *Visio*. Whereas Dante has here presented them as seven horned heads growing out of the monstrously disfigured cart, Langland shows them, more realistically, as making inroads, now stealthily, now brazenly, and always devastatingly, in the hearts of the people. The scene is, on the whole, grotesque rather than tragic, and often borders on the "picaresque":

Sleuth with his slynge an hard saut he made,
Proude prestes come with hym moo than a thousand,
In paltokes and pyked shoes and pisseres longe knyues,
Comen agein Conscience; with Coueityse thei helden.

(B, XX, 216-20)

[Sloth with his sling made a fierce assault,
While more than a thousand proud priests came with him.
With short jackets, pointed shoes, and long daggers like
cutthroats—
They came against Conscience; and they took the side of
Covetousness.]

The real focus of the entire vision, however, is on the progressive
internal disintegration of the Church, culminating ultimately in
complete disruption. This is brought about not so much by the
violent attack of external forces as by an increasing disorientation
in the body of the faithful—among pastors as well as flock—
unable to hold fast to the ideal embodied by Piers, and reluctant
to "redde quod debes" (line 305). The crisis of the Christian
Conscience had started in fact even before the assault of Antichrist
and his army. It was already apparent immediately after Conscience
gathered all Christian people inside the moat of holiness built
around "Unity" in order to defend them against the impending
threat of Pride. What actually undermines the whole spiritual
structure is human ignorance, self-interest, incredulity: many refuse
to "pay what they owe" before receiving Communion, a brewer
proclaims he will keep to his dishonest ways of profit and not
"hakke after holynesse", a "lewed" vicar dispiritedly declares he
knows no cardinal virtues but worldly cardinals from Rome, a
lord makes of *Spiritus Fortitudinis* brute force, and a king egoisti-
cally tramples on *Spiritus Justicie* (B, XX, 388-473). The course
of human wilfulness comes to a head when Hypocrisy breaks
through the defence line of the beleaguered Church and once more
the attempt is made to reconcile the irreconcilable. Men baulk at
the harsh medicine of true repentance, refuse shrift, and turn to
Ease and "sire Lief-to-lyue-in-leccherie" (l. 308). A more accom-
modating surgeon is at hand. Friar Flatter, *penetrans domos,*

gains admittance into the castle, offers "his phisik" of a "pryue
payement",

> And plastered hem so esyly thei drede no synne.
>
> (B, XX, 377)
>
> [And plastered them so mildly (was so lenient in penance)
>   that they dread no sin.]

The fatal blow has been struck inside the Castle of Unity. Once
Contrition is wounded by the cupidity of the Friars, the earthly
Church totters and sadly falls. Then:

> "Bi Cryste," quod Conscience tho, "I wil bicome a pilgryme,
> And walken as wyde as al the worlde lasteth,
> To seke Piers the Plowman that Pryde may destruye,
> And that freres hadde a fyndyng that for nede flateren,
> And contrepleteth me, Conscience; now Kynde me auenge,
> And sende me happe and hele til I haue Piers the Plowman!"
> And sitthe he gradde after grace til I gan awake.
>
> (ibid., 378-84)
>
> ["By Christ," Conscience said then, "I will become a pilgrim,
> And walk to the end of the world while it lasts
> To seek Piers the Plowman who can destroy Pride,
> So that friars who now flatter for their needs
> And oppose me, Conscience, may be provided for;
> And let Nature avenge me, and grant me his help and healing
>   power until I have found Piers Plowman!"
> Then he cried aloud for grace until I awoke.]

Confronted with a spectacle of widespread recklessness and the
rejection by the majority of men of the ideal of perfection, Christian Conscience takes the only course left open and starts with
resolve on a second, unending quest for Piers Plowman.

There is general agreement among recent critics that although the
final Passus of Langland's poem may appear as a gloomy and

tragic anticlimax,[36] the concluding lines, together with a certain measure of despondency,[37] contain a message of great hope and an unshakable determination to go on striving after salvation. And certainly Conscience's cry for grace cannot but confirm such a view. It is, in the midst of darkening clouds, a final corroboration of the validity and necessity of the Redemption for the individual as well as for all mankind. Besides, the call on Nature for vengeance seems to suggest, implicitly, that the defeat is temporary. For a day will come when Piers will be found again to restore Holy Church. From this point of view the close of *Piers Plowman* offers a further instance of analogy with the end of *Purgatory*. Canto XXXIII, the last of the *Commedia's* middle cantica, contains the same twofold message, of warning and of promise. But it is delivered in a more sustained and far intenser tone. In comparison Conscience's last words sound rather subdued and undertoned. The difference, on the other hand, can be explained by the fact that Beatrice, unlike Piers, remains constantly present, dominating the scene from beginning to end. It is she who, in the full assurance of the eternal Church's incorruptibility, allowed the Pilgrim to witness the sight of the corrupted temporal Church:

"Però, in pro del modo che mal vive,
al carro tieni or gli occhi; e quel che vedi,
ritornato di là, fa che tu scrive."

(Purg., XXXII, 103-5)

["Therefore, for the world's good which lives ill,
hold thine eyes now on the car and what thou seest
do thou write when thou hast returned yonder."]

36. This was the view advanced e.g. by C. Dawson, who described the conclusion of *Piers Plowman* as "a final battle for a lost cause against the unloosed hosts of hell", adding then that "... it is characteristic of the Nordic strain in Langland's poetry, that his epic should end, like the Volospa and the epics of the heathen north, on a note of defeat and despair" ("The Vision of P.P." in *Medieval Religion and Other Studies,* Part III, London 1934, pp. 161-3).

37. Professor Kane, op. cit., p. 244, writes in this respect that the poem "develops ... to a last ideal which seems to the poet so high that he as much as acknowledges the impossibility of attaining it, and thus brings his search to an end".

And it is she who, after lamenting with the seven Nymphs the devastation of Jerusalem, became so sad "that scarce more changed was Mary at the cross" (XXXIII, 6). Then,

> ... levata in piè,
> rispose, colorata come foco:
> "*Modicum et non videbitis me;*
> *et iterum,* sorelle mie dilette,
> *modicum et vos videbitis me!*"
>
> (ibid., 8-12)

[... rising erect on her feet and glowing like fire: "*Modicum, et non videbitis me; et iterum,* my beloved sisters, *modicum, et vos videbitis me.*"]

The words spoken by Christ to announce his death and resurrection tell of the Church's momentary eclipse and the certainty of its return. In the meantime divine punishment will inexorably fall upon those who have desecrated the temple and spoiled, for a second time, the tree of mankind:

> "Sappi che 'l vaso che 'l serpente ruppe
> fu e non è, ma chi n'ha colpa, creda
> che vendetta di Dio non teme suppe."
>
> (ibid., 34-6)

["Know that the vessel the serpent broke was and is not, but let him that has the blame be assured that God's vengenace fears no sop."]

The time is near, continues Beatrice, when "a five hundred ten and five" (ibid., 43) will come to restore order by killing "the thief and the giant" (ibid., 44-5). No amount of hermeneutic ingenuity has so far succeeded in unravelling the mystery of the identity of the "one" Dante had in mind. Like the Greyhound of *Inferno I* who would come to destroy the she-wolf, this is a God-sent personage, who sums up in himself all the poet's hopes for the regeneration of Christendom.[38] Beatrice's words are as purposely dark as they are strongly resolute. Her "enigma forte" (line 50) may not be easily solved in the present time, but it is meant, all the same, to strengthen her devotee's faith in herself and in the ineluctable events she foretells.

The disturbing questions which would, expectedly, arise from the vision of the Church sadly marred and all but ruined, have been answered in a diverse but not so dissimilar way by the two poets. At the end of his expiatory course, when the hard-won spiritual rehabilitation has been achieved, Dante the traveller has returned for a short while to the initial situation of moral confusion—the "selva selvaggia" haunted by the she-wolf. In the picture of the Church fornicating with the kings of the earth he has seen more clearly the ultimate example of cupidity's destructive power.[39] These ills will not be without end, nor without retribution. Dante's stand is expressed in such decisive, unequivocal terms. Similarly Langland's Dreamer, after witnessing the wonders of Christ's Redemption, from the loftiness of contemplation has descended to the world of actuality, the Field Full of Folk portrayed in the Prologue and in the *Visio,* that is contemporary society where Lady Meed reigned supreme. Enlightened by all that he has experienced since, he sees once more, and with more understanding, the source of human corruption, and how cupidity has come near to undoing both Church and society.[40] But, unlike

38. Undoubtedly the "515" prophesied by Beatrice is the same as the *Veltro* prophesied by Virgil in the Prologue of the *Commedia.* Whether the poet intended an ideal emperor or a pope we do not know, simply because, most probably, Dante did not know himself. He could therefore express the certainty of his advent by indicating the "one" with a numerical cipher, in harmony with the apocalyptic inspiration of these last cantos. See for the whole question Pietrobono, op. cit., p. 450.

39. We have no direct reference to the she-wolf of *Inf.* I in the vision of the Church's corruption. But that Dante had it in mind here seems more than evident. See F. Tocco, "Lettura del C. XXXII del Purgatorio" in *Letture Dantesche a cura di G. Getto,* p. 1326.

40. Cf. Kane, op. cit., p. 246. It must be recognized that, in structural terms, the diffuse, largely circumstantial account of the evils besetting fourteenth-century England corresponds to the initial stages of Langland's poem more clearly and more designedly than Dante's recalling of the beginning of *Inferno* at the end of *Purgatorio.*

the Pilgrim of *Purgatorio*, he now hears no voice of outright condemnation of those responsible for the Church's downfall, no strong appeal to divine justice to crush the wickedest among the clergy, only a sincere desire, a pious hope for the reform of the Friars. Together with Conscience he can only embark on a renewed search for that Piers who has vanished but must be found again whenever men of good will, under the guidance of this Christ-like figure, will want to realize in themselves righteousness and, above it, holiness. Langland's confidence in man's capacity to achieve salvation is as positive as Dante's,[41] but it is balanced by a deep awareness that the struggle with Antichrist must go on as long as life lasts. The conclusion of *Piers Plowman*, like most of the final Passus, is in the words of R. W. Frank "moralistic rather than prophetic, realistic rather than mystical".[42] Such a strong sense of realism is further evidenced by the half whimsical, half tragic portrayal of the Dreamer: here is a man (the poet himself?) painfully conscious of the frailty of his existence, gouty, toothless, impotent, and approaching death. In spite of the cumulative wisdom acquired during so long years of dreaming, he finds himself very much awake to pressing bodily needs:

"How shal I come to catel so, to clothe me and to fede?"

(B, **XX**, 208)

["How shall I get wealth to clothe and feed myself?"]

The answer, given already in the previous line, is clear, definite, and uplifting:

"Lerne to loue", quod Kynde, "and leue of alle othre."

(line 207)

["Learn to love," said Nature, "and give up everything else."]

41. Equally strong is Langland's faith in the renewal of Christian society. But it is not expressed here. It is "sounded" much earlier in the poem when Conscience, anticipating the downfall of Meed, foresees the coming of a messianic kingdom of truth, peace and love (cf. B, III, 282-90). A generous Utopia, this, that echoes Dante's prophecy of the Veltro (*Inf.* 106-11). See above, Chapter 2, pp. 40-1; 54-5.
42. Op. cit., p. 118.

The same sobering feeling about life's brevity hangs over the close of the *Purgatorio,* but it is accompanied by the consciousness of the high prophetic mission Dante has accepted and to which he has devoted his art:

> "Tu nota; e sì come da me son porte,
>   così queste parole segna ai vivi
>   del viver ch'è un correre alla morte."

(Purg., XXXIII, 52-4)

["Take note, and even as these words are uttered by me so teach them to those who live the life that is a race to death."]

Beatrice's reminder of death, after all, coincides with the beginning of the true life, into which the poet-pilgrim is about to be launched and where she will assist in the fulfilment of the Love she has revealed to him. In the midst of the uncertainty caused by the storming of Antichrist our Dreamer also has been confirmed in this same Love. His whole being is now definitely orientated towards the ideal which perhaps only God's "Fools" can attain. But it is only of "orientation" we can speak. The presence of the narrow limits of this life and the awareness of human frailty prevent our poet-dreamer from launching into the full realization of it.

A recent critic of *Piers Plowman* at the end of a brilliant introduction to the poem suggests that: ". . . the idea of the search beginning once more has, in more important ways, a great optimism in it. It may symbolize the renewed effort to establish proper contact between man and Christ, the renewed effort to live the good moral life, *to embark upon the intimate journey to God in the stillness of contemplation and to bring others the fruit of that journey.*"[43] The truth of the first half of this remark is irrefutable;

43. E. Salter, op. cit., p. 104. Italics mine. Professor Donaldson's attitude is more guarded and sensible; in this respect he writes: "As it stands, *Dobest* does not seem to contain much that is suggestive of the vision of God of St. Bernard. Nevertheless, in the section as it stands there are elements suggestive of the unitive condition of the soul, just as in B's Do-well there is a good deal about patience and in B's Do-bet the main theme is charity. Specifically, there is the constant repetition of the word *unity,* even though it usually signifies the Church. But I am unable to make much out of this. Progress along the anagogic path is, of course, a gift of grace, both in Bernard and in *Piers Plowman*" (op. cit., p. 197).

the second part constitutes a stimulating reflection which would require a great deal of ingenuity to prove. But if it is so, it remains, as regards Langland, a declaration of intention, the premise of a higher mental and poetical flight which can be found, fully realized, in Dante, and only in Dante among the medieval poets who have dealt with matters human and divine. Langland has his Inferno and his Purgatorio. He does not give us a Paradiso, nor did he intend to. Perhaps he could not.

CHAPTER 5

ALLEGORY AS INCARNATION IN DANTE AND LANGLAND

The foregoing comparative analysis has enabled us to highlight some important correspondences in the structural patterns of the two poems. While focusing attention on the resemblance between the central issues of *Piers,Plowman* and those of the *Divine Comedy* I have endeavoured to omit all particular considerations of an artistic or, more precisely, an aesthetic nature. Only incidentally, when a particular episode or image warranted it, did I enlarge very briefly, and rather casually, on their respective poetic value. Yet no comparative study, however limited and introductory, would be satisfactory if it did not extend to some relevant aspects of poetic expression. One should not, in my opinion, be discouraged or even put off from attempting this by Professor Bloomfield's remark regarding Dante and Langland that "the difference in poetical ability between the two poets is obvious".[1] Such an assertion needs to be qualified. If we take it in its general implication there is no great difficulty in accepting it. But if we restrict it to some limited modes of expression or imaginative aspects we cannot agree as to its absolute validity. All depends on which particular field we choose to see the "ability" of each poet realized. Langland is sublime or powerful in his own right and in his own manner. As often noted by exegetes, and even by the common reader, his picture of the suffering poor (C, X, 71-97) is profoundly moving, and in its own kind unsurpassed. Christ's speech to Satan in the scene of the Harrowing of Hell (B, XVIII, 325-76), or Repentance's prayer following the Confession scene in Passus V (lines 485-513), can be identified as outstanding examples of poetic

1. "The Present State of Piers Plowman Studies" in *Speculum*, XIV, (April 1939), p. 215.

power and depth. But while recognizing Langland's achievement in these or other instances, we cannot make use of them as grounds for a possible comparison with passages in Dante—or any other poet for that matter—unless such examples can be paralleled in tone or content. And this does not seem to hold here. And when we are told that Langland's "power of rendering imaginable what before was only intelligible is nowhere, not even in Dante, better exemplified than in Langland's lines on the Incarnation",[2] we must be wary; first, we must verify whether in Dante there are lines on the same or a comparable subject (which is the case), and then compare and contrast them. In the end we may discover that in Dante the treatment is quite different.[3] In order, therefore, to assess the respective merits of the two poets, the choice of a specific, restricted, and common topic is essential. This would help greatly towards an effective appraisal of the "poetical essence" displayed by each of them. I would like to examine in particular some motifs common to the *Commedia* and *Piers Plowman;* for example the portrayal of certain major characters and images. Such an analysis, in fact, impinges directly on the problem of allegory versus poetry or, if one prefers it, poetry versus allegory. I think the problem can be best introduced by a remark concerning Dante made by Etienne Gilson, the distinguished historian of medieval philosophy, who cannot be suspected of "aesthetical" prejudices. His judgement is too sound for that. I quote at length:

"If the sacred poem still lives, it is because its creator has peopled it only with living beings. Himself in the first place, by a unique decision which no poet had ever dared to take or has ever taken since. Then all the others, for not only have all the characters that move in it lived in history or legend, but they live in the poem more intensely than ever, in their individual essence as finally manifested by the inflexible law of divine justice. There is not a single dead man in the whole of the *Divine Comedy*. That is why

2. C. S. Lewis, *Allegory of Love*, p. 160.
3. Langland's well-known lines on the Incarnation are in B, I, 151-6 (see also: B, XX, 39-46). For Dante cf. *Par.*, VII, 25-61. Here Beatrice expounds in a reasoned, calm tone the mystery of the Incarnation in answer to Dante's question why God had chosen this means to save mankind. It is strictly doctrinal, without any use of metaphor or imagery.

the text of Dante has nothing in common with any *Pélerinage de Vie Humaine, Roman de la Rose,* or other allegorical rubbish with its poverty of human stuff. When people tell us that 'the *Roman de la Rose* ought to be studied here[4] as Dante Alighieri is studied in the institutes of Rome and Tuscany', they are simply and solely confusing art with philology. When Jean de Meun chances to tell us of Charlemagne, Abelard and Heloise, we fall greedily upon these drops of water in his desert of allegories, but Slander, Giving-too-much, and Mad Bounty soon reassert their rights and Jean's few profoundly human lines on Guillaume de Lorris and on himself are quickly buried beneath the chatter of Fear, Shame, Danger and Hypocrisy. The adventures of these proper names leave us cold and we no longer read what they say because it is completely and utterly insipid, but we shall always read Dante because the *Divine Comedy* is the story of a living being in the midst of other living beings . . ."[5]

Clearly here the line is drawn neatly between conventional allegory which would seem to hold no claim to being real literature, and literature proper or what has been defined as "incarnational literature" with a Shakespearian connotation.[6] Where should we place *Piers Plowman* in the light of Gilson's views? Must we include its allegorical characters among those who act or speak in an "utterly insipid" manner? Certainly not; firstly, because even though many, perhaps the majority, belong to the "Giving-too-much" and "Mad Bounty" category,[7] quite a substantial number of Langland's characterizations are endowed with a remarkable poetical energy; secondly, because together with abstract types we find in the poem a whole host of real, flesh-and-blood characters, observed in a dream but drawn from life. This fact

4. In France, I suppose.
5. *Dante the Philosopher,* pp. 72-3.
6. Cf. Graham Hough, "The Allegorical Circle" in *Critical Quarterly,* Vol. 3 (Autumn 1961), pp. 199-209. "Incarnational literature is that in which any 'abstract' content is completely absorbed in character and action and completely expressed in them" (ibid., p. 205).
7. This would include what has been called "sign-post allegories" which Langland has in common with other allegorists. See Dunning, *The A Text of Piers Plowman,* p. 134.

leads us to the vexed question of symbolism and personification in allegorical works, which becomes even more complicated when they occur in relation to each other within one poem. Not long ago Professor R. Frank Jr. advanced the view that, for the sake of clarity, a necessary distinction must be made in defining poems of an allegorical nature and, significantly for our problem, suggested calling "Dante's type of allegory *symbol-allegory* and Langland's type *personification-allegory*".[8] Professor Frank's division of the two *genres* is welcome in as far as it satisfies the need to arrive at, and maintain, a theoretical understanding of different forms. But, I am sure, he did not mean, as Mrs. Salter has suggested,[9] to exclude any possible association of *Piers Plowman* with the *Divine Comedy*. In fact, Frank is perfectly aware, on the one hand, that the two devices can coexist in one poem, as they do in *Piers Plowman,* and, on the other, he declares that he is primarily concerned with the "exegesis of the personification-allegory and not with the aesthetics of the form".[10] The formula therefore cannot be interpreted too rigidly and must necessarily be applied in an elastic way. If the great majority of characters in the *Commedia,* together with many objects or events, are symbolical of a spiritual or moral reality, there are others which, as personifications of abstract ideas, can, and just as effectively, convey an important meaning in the context of a scene or situation. Take a classic example: the cardinal and theological virtues in the pageant described in the last cantos of *Purgatorio*. Conversely, if a good many *dramatis personae* in *Piers Plowman* are personifications of abstract entities—like Lady Meed and Holy Church or Thought, Wit, Study and so on—some of the most significant are symbolical personages who, from their early, direct, simple and literal presentation, accumulate the highest meaning in the course of the poem.

8. "The Art of Reading Medieval Personification Allegory", *E.L.H.,* XX, 1953, p. 238.

9. *Piers Plowman, An Introduction,* p. 77 (in a footnote reference to Frank's essay).

10. Frank, art. cit., p. 247. Professor Frank's purpose is simply to help the reader to build up the necessary mental attitude in order to grasp what the poet or poets want to communicate and to get familiarized with the form. It is a question of distinction and not of absolute opposition.

Piers is a symbol, and the central one of the poem, and can easily join hands with Abraham, Moses and the Samaritan, or the Emperor Trajan. Undoubtedly, in adopting a whole series of human figures, historical or legendary, in order to illustrate ideal states of vice or virtue, Dante has the advantage over most medieval authors of developing a "symbolic speech" which lends itself quite naturally to depicting dramatic situations. The symbol and the parabolic speech are constituent elements of the literal narrative[11] and the passage to a deeper insight or meaning could even be dispensed with by the reader who is fully impressed by the direct impact of the image. This is particularly true of the *Inferno*.[12] But the objective dramatization realized through the perception of the concrete and varied manifestations of sinfulness (as in the incidents of the exploratory journey) should not stop us from seeing the second, or deeper, meaning which is "contained" simultaneously in the figure itself. The moral application yields itself to us through the import of the particular situation, and not by means of extensive or explicit moralizing. It may be that we come to realize the full *significatio* of Hell in the second stage of the journey, when the "didactic" activity of the Pilgrim's Guide and the "lessons" learned from the penitent spirits will put it in the right perspective and thus reveal its meaning.[13] And so it is

11. For an interesting, exhaustive discussion on these problems see A. Pagliaro, "Simbolo e Allegoria nella Divina Commedia" in *L'Alighieri* (*Rassegna bibliografica dantesca*), 2, Roma 1963, pp. 3-35.
12. Cf. the significant statement by Coleridge. "The Divina Commedia is a system of moral, political, and theological truths, with arbitrary personal exemplifications, which are not, in my opinion, allegorical. I do not even feel convinced that the punishments in the Inferno are strictly allegorical. I rather take them to have been in Dante's mind *quasi*-allegorical, or conceived in analogy to pure allegory" (*The Literary Remains of S. T. Coleridge* collected and edited by H. N. Coleridge, Vol. I, London 1836, p. 157). While this makes a non-allegorical reading quite adequate, it does not, of course, exclude allegorical inferences. A more recent example of a quasi-allegorical approach to the *Comedy* is the outstanding work of E. Auerbach, *Dante Poet of the Secular World* (Transl. R. Manheim), Chicago 1961.
13. This is the purpose of the great discourse of Virgil on love (*Purg.*, XVII-XVIII) as the main spring-force of all human actions which, when misplaced or perverted, constitutes the cause of every sinful behaviour. Cf. F. Fergusson, op. cit., p. 130.

from the scrutiny of the "centre" of the *Commedia* that we come to understand—within and beyond the exemplification of punishment by divine justice—the mistaken movement of the spirit. Francesca and her lover (*Inf.*, V) in the sweeping force of their mutual passion and the end to which the headlong urge of their senses bring them signify also, and perhaps primarily, the perversion of courtly love. Farinata degli Uberti (canto X), the apparently much admired municipal leader, incarnates—we now appreciate—the blinding passion of party-politics, and Pier delle Vigne (canto XIII) symbolizes the painful limits of human activity turned exclusively towards the values of the earthly city. Similarly Brunetto Latini (canto XV) embodies in himself the inadequacy of a rationalistic culture which is an end in itself; and splendid as this culture may appear, it does not excuse but rather makes more disgusting his vice of sodomy, in spite of all Dante's pitying undertones. And in Ulysses the poet will represent the tragic result of a mistaken "virtute e conoscenza" by which man, relying blindly on his own powers, challenges, perhaps inadvertently, the ordinances of Providence. And so on down through the variegated succession of live beings who signify this or that aspect of wrong-doing. Together with the allied elements of their environment and with the monstrous figures around them, they point, allegorically, to a corresponding state of a turning from righteousness in men still on this side of the grave—and this is exactly in accordance with the poet's intention.[14]

Now, I would suggest that in *Piers Plowman* we can detect the same process leading precisely to the same result, but one that is achieved by an inverse method. Langland's allegorical method is, in a way, the reverse of Dante's. In general he presents his abstract typification of a moral quality or attitude in such realistic characterizations as naturally lend themselves to lively and intense dramatization. I do not mean that there is a "gradual passage" from an immaterial appellation to an intensified lifelikeness. For such an adherence to life in Langland's characters is often incorporated in them from their very first appearance. This immediacy of visual

14. Cf. Letter to Cangrande, paragraph 8.

perception, incidentally, parallels the distinctive quality of Langland's poetic language, which is capable of giving concreteness to abstract concepts concerning mysteries of Faith or moral truths.[15] As regards his personifications, however, it must be observed that the translation of an idea into a viable sensible image or character does not materialize in the same degree in all of them—which is the same as to say that it is not realized with evident consistency throughout the poem. In the *Visio* for instance the poet sometimes is so much taken by his picturing of a vivid scene from human experience that the allegorical characters are crowded into the action in such a way as to prevent any possibility of a full measure of individualization. The point can be illustrated by the following example :

> Ac Symonie and Cyuile and sisoures of courtes
> Were moste pryue with Mede of any men, me thoughte.
> Ac Fauel was the first that fette hire out of boure,
> And as a brokour broughte hir to be with Fals enioigned.
> Whan Symonye and Cyuile seigh here beire wille,
> Thei assented for siluer to sei as bothe wolde.
> Thanne lepe Lyer forth, and seide "lo here! a chartre,
> That Gyle with his gret othes gaf hem togidere",
> And preide Cyuile to se and Symonye to rede it.
> Thanne Symonye and Cyuile stonden forth bothe,
> And vnfoldeth the feffement that Fals hath ymaked,
> And thus bigynneth thes gomes to greden ful heigh.
>
> (B, II, 62-73)

> [But Simony and Civil Law and jurors of courts
> Were, of all men, most intimate with Meed, it seemed to me.
> But Flattery was the first to fetch her out of her chamber,
> And as a matchmaker brought her out to be joined in marriage with Falsehood.
> When Simony and Civil Law understood the wish of both of them,
> They agreed, in return for money. to say whatever they both wished.

15. Cf. Kane, op. cit., pp. 237-8.

Then Liar leaped out and said: "Behold, here is a charter
That Guile, with his great oaths, has given them both",
And he begged Civil Law to look it over and Simony to read it.
Whereupon both Simony and Civil Law both stand up
And unfold the deed of endowment that Falsehood had
    drawn up,
And so these fellows begin to read it at the top of their
    voices.]

In a dozen lines the author has managed to gather five or six
representatives of the forces that corrupt society. There is life,
movement in it, and by visualizing their "concerted" action the
poet succeeds in conveying his meaning. The same consideration
applies to the description of the march to Westminster (ibid., 161-
87) where the quick tempo of the action, while revealing in
vividly pictorial language the poet's intention, hardly permits
isolating Flattery, Fraud, Civil and Guile from sheriffs, notaries
or Pauline Friars. Yet it is these "abstractions" which stand out
more sharply than the apparently human figures. The relative
anonymity of ordinary men in this context is designedly maintained. It shows effectively how much they are subject to the
powerful influences exerted by the forces which condition their
behaviour. When, however, the poet's emotional or satiric impulse
is directed to a particular situation, his allegorical creatures come
to life in a more distinct and convincing presentation—as with
Liar at the end of Passus II, or with Peace and Wrong in their
litigation at court. When a harried innocent complains in factual
terms of a bullying rascal, nothing is left to abstraction but the
names:

And thanne come Pees into parlement and put forth a bille,
How Wronge ageines his wille had his wyf taken,
And how he rauisshed Rose Reginoldes loue,
And Margarete of hir maydenhode maugre here chekis.
"Bothe my gees and my grys his gadelynges feccheth;
I dar noughte for fere of hym fyghte ne chyde.
. . . .

He meyneteneth his men to morther myne hewen,
Forstalleth my feyres and fighteth in my chepynge,
And breketh vp my bernes dore and bereth awey my whete."

(B, IV, 47-52; 55-7)

[Then Peace came into Parliament and lodged a complaint,
That Wrong had abducted his wife against his will,
And that he had ravished Rose, Reginald's girl,
And deprived Margaret of her virginity in spite of all her
    resistance.
"His ruffians seize my geese and my pigs;
I dare not fight or quarrel with him because I am scared.
. . . .
He aids and abets his men in murdering my servants,
He forestalls me at fairs and upsets my bargaining,
Breaks down my barn door and carries off my wheat."]

Of Lady Meed and her dramatic confrontation with the king,
Conscience, and Reason enough has been said already with regard
to their significant interrelationship in the structural development
of the poem. Here we might add that no matter how decisive the
role played by the latter two in the thematic resolution of the
Visio, they are and remain flat personified abstractions, hardly
worked up to a fully artistic characterization.[16] By this I mean
the absence in them of even that half-way "humanization" which
could make their "image" more compelling. And certainly it is to
Langland's great credit that he has kept them lively by the force
of the argument they carry on with great dialectic skill, thus
avoiding the danger of presenting them as frigid cardboard
figures.[17] Things are quite different with Lady Meed. In her theme

16. I cannot agree with Professor Lawlor's view that the poet's visualizing
power is equally well exemplified by Conscience's kneeling in front of the
king "when the balance of argument sways dangerously against him", op.
cit., p. 262. A simple physical bending of knees is too scant a detail to confer realism on this allegorical character.

17. The same applies to the personifications of mental faculties in *Dowel*
and *Dobet,* although they demonstrate a considerable psychological penetration on the part of the poet.

and image are fused in sharper visual relief than in the case of any other "actor" in the *Visio*. The notions of bribery and reward, the complex, all too human predicament involved in the problem of legitimate gain and wrongful profiteering, which lead to a final unrelenting revelation of a many-sided incarnation of cupidity, are skilfully moulded into a most plausible character. All the external and internal attributes of a female figure, now irresistibly alluring, now shamelessly deceitful, are so convincingly built into her as to defy any attempt to define her either as an abstraction personified or a symbolic personage. More appropriately perhaps she is a perfect combination of both; or, beyond that, even a real woman, as we can see for instance when, abandoned momentarily by her former supporters, she is shown defenceless in the fragility of her being:

> Alle fledden for fere and flowen in-to hernes,
> Saue Mede the mayde na mo durst abide.
> Ac trewli to telle she trembled for drede,
> And ek wept and wronge whan she was attached.
> (B, II, 233-6)[18]
> [All fled in terror and flew into hiding-places,
> No one, except Meed the Maiden, dared to stay there.
> But to tell the truth she trembled with fear
> And also wept and wrung her hands when she was arrested.]

But it is with the representation of the Deadly Sins that Langland, as one has by now come to expect, exhibits a profounder insight into human experience. As is often remarked by students of *Piers Plowman* and easily recognized by every reader, the poet's resourcefulness reveals itself here in terms of "visual imagination".[19]

18. Langland's characterization of Lady Meed acquires, of course, still greater plausibility from the possible connection with Alice Perrers. This was already noted by Skeat in the *Commentary to the Text of Piers Plowman*, Vol. II, Notes on p. 31. See also M. McKisack, "The XIV Century" in *Oxford History of England*, 1959, p. 390.
19. As Professor Kane has observed. "This quality in him (Langland) has not been sufficiently remarked; it is stronger and clearer even than Chaucer's, and functions with unbroken ease even when he is dealing with allegorical characters" (op. cit., p. 236).

Quite naturally therefore the presence of this traditional theme both in Dante and Langland invites comparison. This, in my opinion, can be better worked out by the stressing of relevant pictorial qualities in single images than by attending unduly to diverse elements of setting and structural positioning. For our purpose examples must in the main be confined to the Confession Scene in Passus V; these should be dealt with chiefly in relation to the sinful dispositions in *Purgatorio*. However, in order to adduce some significant parallels, even by way of contrast, it will be convenient, not to say necessary, to refer to other episodes in both poems.

At Reason's behest the Capital Sins, mouthpieces of the people summoned to repentance, come forward to make their confessions. The first is Pride. But the self-humiliating protestations of "Peronelle Proude-herte" (B, V, 63-71) are too scanty to permit a tangible presentation of *Superbia*. For that we must turn to the anonymous figure which springs from Haukyn's stained coat,

"in   aparaille   and   in   porte   proude   amonges   the   peple"
[in   dress   and   bearing   haughty   among   the   people]
boasting and bragging

        with many bolde othes
And in-obedient to ben vndernome of any lyf lyuynge,
And so syngulere by hym-self as to syghte of the people,
Was no suche as hym-self ne none so pope-holy.

                (B, XIII, 278; 281-4)

   [with many a blasphemous oath
And unwilling to be reproved by any living man,
So unique in himself in the sight of the people:
There was no one quite like him nor so utterly hypocritical.]

He is the quintessence of overweening egotism, scornful of his fellow-creatures, domineering, and claiming first place in song and sport. Everybody must know

"What I suffred and seighe and some tymes hadde,
And what I couth and knewe and what kynne I come of."

(ibid., 310-11)

["How much I suffered and what I saw and how much one
    time I possessed,
And what I understood and was able to do and what a distin-
    guished kin I came of."]

This vivid personification of hauteur and vainglory, pitilessly
exposed by the poet between the lines, in its sheer vacuity and
falsity reminds us of the identical moral posture engraved by
Dante in the vigorous profiles of some proud penitents. Even more
than the "visible parlare" of the iconography depicting various
examples of the vice or its opposite virtue, it is the psychology of
the personages met on the first ledge which reveals the essential
nature of Pride. Outstanding among them is Umberto Aldobran-
deschi, who from beneath his crushing burden of stone seems to
stir once more "nella plastica alterigia della sua vita terrena": [20]

"Io fui latino e nato d'un gran Tosco:
    Guglielmo Aldobrandesco fu mio padre;
    non so se 'l nome suo già mai fu vosco.
L'antico sangue e l'opere leggiadre
    de' miei maggiori mi fer sì arrogante,
    che non pensando alla comune madre,
ogni uomo ebbi a dispetto tanto avante,
    ch'io ne mori', come, i Sanesi sanno
    e sallo in Campagnatico ogni fante."

(Purg., **XI,** 58-66)

["I was Italian, and born of a great Tuscan.
Guglielmo Aldobrandesco was my father,
I know not if his name was ever heard among you.
The ancient blood and gallant deeds of
my ancestors made me so arrogant that, forgetful
of our common mother, I carried my scorn of every
man so far that I died for it—how, the Sienese
know and every child in Campagnatico."]

20. Momigliano, op. cit., p. 341.

The relative analogy between the representations that we can detect in the above images cannot be established with regard to the exemplifications of Lust. Langland's portrayal of the vice is shorter but far intenser than for the rest of the Deadly Sins. In its graphic concision and concrete detail it lays bare the desperate plight of the human creatures who, as Dante would say,

> la ragion sommettono al talento.
>
> (Inf., VI, 39)
>
> [submit reason to desire.]

The passage is found most fully in the C Text of *Piers Plowman*,[21] and must be quoted *in extenso*:

> "To eche maide that ich mette ich made hure a sygne
> Semynge to synne-warde and somme gan ich taste
> Aboute the mouthe, and by-nythe by-gan ich to grope,
> Til oure bothers wil was on; to werke we yeden
> As wel fastyngdaies as Frydaies and heye-feste euenes,
> As luf in lente as oute of lente alle tymes liche—
> Such werkus with ous were neuere out of seson—
> Til we myghte no more; thanne hadde we murye tales
> Of puterie and of paramours and proueden thorw speches,
> Handlynge and halsynge and al-so thorw cussynge
> Excitynge oure aither other til oure olde synne;
> . . . .
> Whenne ich was old and hor and hadde lore that kynde,
> Ich had lykynge to lauhe of lecherous tales.
> Now, lord, for thy leaute of lechours haue mercy!"
>
> (C, VII, 178-88; 193-5)
>
> ["To each maiden I met I gave a sign
> Suggesting sin, and some I kissed
> On the mouth, and fumbled under their clothes,
> Until we both desired the same thing; to work we went
> On fasting-days as well as Fridays and on the vigils of feast-
>   days,

21. In B it is included in the episode of Haukyn (XIII, 344-52).

As willingly in Lent as out of Lent, at all times the same—
Such acts with us were never out of season—
Until we were sated; then we would tell merry tales
Of lechery and of paramours and commit sin with our words,
Touching and embracing and kissing also,
Exciting each other till we'd commit the old sin.

. . . .

When I was old and hoary and had lost that power,
I had pleasure in laughing at lecherous tales.
Now, Lord, since you are faithful (to your assurance of
   mercy), have pity on lechers."]

It would seem improper, even unpardonably harsh, to compare these lines with those in which the immortal Francesca tells her story in *Inferno* V. Yet the famous episode is the only possible example available for comparative reference,[22] when looking at the image of Lust in *Piers,* if only to illustrate the contrasting power of the poets. Without quoting Dante directly, we can observe that, in spite of the common elements of the shuddering of the flesh and mutual sexual indulgence, or the mention of the tempting reading of romances of love, the representations of the sin could not be more diametrically opposed. In Dante we have the pathos of a sinful love—delicately presented in the fine shading of sentiment and instinct, but with no suggestion of animal degradation: which makes Francesca's confession almost unbearably poignant. In Langland, instead, we have the most vigorously naturalistic portrayal of a lecherous individual, quivering with the sensual passion of youth and growing into an almost obscene image of a senile obsession, which is hard to conceive as being redeemed by the final cry for mercy.

The confessions of Envy, Anger, Avarice, Gluttony and Sloth supply, as is well known, the best evidence of Langland's unequalled flair for visual and dramatic concreteness in the illustration of the sins. A lengthy analysis of the detail of these charac-

22. In *Purgatorio* Lust, referred to as the "peccato ermafrodito", is mentioned by the penitents within the purifying flames of the last terrace. There is no concrete feature illustrating the sin. See canto XXVI.

terizations is not called for here. All of them, after all, repeat the same pattern of physical features and overt manifestations in actions and words which, developed to the extreme limit of caricature, succeed in highlighting their characteristic qualities. Without elaborating on what many others have said in this respect regarding Langland,[23] I wish to point out that, in many ways, such a technique possesses the descriptive energy with which Dante renders, penetratingly, the nature of the various vices both in *Inferno* and *Purgatorio;* although here the details of each picture are inseparable from the notion either of fitting punishment or the appropriate atmosphere. The allegorical illustration of Envy, for example, is introduced by Dante in a series of physical details which are meant to convey, together with the pitiful, almost repellent mode of the torment, the moral quality of the sin. On the cornice of the Mountain the barren bank is "painted"

> col livido color de la petraia.
>   *(Purg.,* XIII, 9)
> [with the livid colour of the stone.]

As he looks over, the Pilgrim sees

> ombre con manti
> al color de la pietra non diversi.
> . . . .
> Di vil cilicio mi parean coperti,
>   e l'un sofferia l'altro con la spalla,
>   e tutti da la ripa eran sofferti.
>   (ibid., 47-8; 58-60)
> [shades with cloaks
> not differing in colour from the stone.
> . . . .
> They appeared to me to be covered with coarse hair-cloth
> and the one supported the other with his shoulder,
> and all were supported by the bank.]

23. See e.g. Lawlor, op. cit., pp. 47-50, for a comprehensive, up to date summary of criticism in this regard.

The attention of the reader will be caught entirely by the sight of the sufferers whose eyelids are sewn together by wire, in total blindness. But it is the leaden colour of the rock, closely matched by the grey roughness of the sack-cloth, which suggests, visually, the lividness of envy. *Invidia's* garments in *Piers* appear strikingly similar and are meant, I believe, to indicate the same moral state, while added physical elements reveal, in a livelier manner, the full potentiality of the vice:

> He was as pale as a pelet in the palsye he semed,
> And clothed in a caurimaury I couthe it noughte discreue;
> In kirtel and kourteby and a knyf bi his syde,
> Of a freres frokke were the forsleues.
> And as a leke hadde yleye longe in the sonne,
> So loked he with lene chekes lourynge foule.
>
> (B, V, 78-83)

> [He was as pale as a stone, and seemed to be suffering from palsy,
> And he was clothed in a coarse cloth which I am unable to describe properly;
> With an under-jacket and a rough tunic, and a knife by his side,
> The foresleeves were cut from a friar's cloak.
> Like a leek that had lain long in the sun,
> So he looked, scowling foully, with shrivelled cheeks.]

The extensive account of the envious man's deeds. his venom in detraction and slander, the writhing bitterness at other people's better lot, which "greueth" him "ful sore", seem to echo the feelings of the Sienese Sapia who, in the midst of her confession, re-lives the malice of her old sin:

> Savia non fui, avvegna che Sapia
>   fossi chiamata, e fui de li altrui danni
>   più lieta assai che di ventura mia.
>
> (*Purg.*, XIII, 109-11)

[Sapient I was not though I was called
Sapia, and I rejoiced far more at others'
hurt than at my own good fortune.]

Burning with hatred for her countrymen (she had been banished
from Siena for unknown reasons), she bore such feelings of jealousy against them as to pray God for their defeat at the hands of
the Florentines:

Rotti fuor quivi e volti ne li amari
    passi di fuga; e veggendo la caccia,
    letizia presi a tutte altre dispari,
tanto che io volsi in su l'ardita faccia,
    gridando a Dio: "omai più non ti temo!"

(ibid., 118-22)

[There they were routed and turned back
in the bitter steps of flight, and seeing
the chase I was filled with gladness beyond
all bounds, so that I turned upward my
bold face, crying to God: "Now I fear Thee no more!"]

Guido del Duca's self-accusation in the following canto repeats an
identical motif, although his envy does not rise to the blasphemous
pitch of Sapia's words:

Fu il mio sangue d'invidia sì riarso,
    che se veduto avessi uom farsi lieto,
    visto m'avresti di livore sparso.

(*Purg.*, XIV, 82-4)

[So inflamed with envy was my blood that if
I had seen a man make merry thou hadst seen
me suffused with livid colour.]

A comparable malicious attitude runs through the grudging, ill-
willed words of Langland's Envy, forming a clear parallel to the
utterances of the penitent just quoted:

And whan I come to the kirke and sholde knele to the rode,
And preye for the poeple as the prest techeth,
For pilgrimes and for palmers for alle the people after,
Thanne I crye on my knees that Cryste gif hem sorwe
That beren away my bolle and my broke schete.

. . . .

And of mennes lesynge I laughe that liketh myn herte;
And for her wynnynge I wepe and waille the tyme.

                          (B, V, 104-8; 112-13)

[And when I come to the church and should kneel in front of
     the cross,
And pray for my neighbours, as the priest teaches,
For pilgrims and palmers and all the rest of the people,
Then on my knees I call out to Christ to bring sorrow
To those who bear away by bowl and my ragged sheet.

. . . .

And I gloat over other men's losses, for that pleases my heart;
But I weep and wail all the time if they make gains.]

Langland's personification may not possess the directness of
impact which derives from the circumstantial stories of historical
characters. But no one can deny that the description of his
behaviour and feelings strikes home with equal intensity. The
evident element of comedy contained in lines 107-8 could not be
farther from Sapia's tragic prayer for the downfall of her fellow-
citizens; but *Invidia's* gloating over other men's losses and his
bewailing their gains conveys to the modern mind, with even
greater immediacy than the words of Dante's character, the sordid
meanness of the vice:

I wolde be gladder, bi god, that Gybbe had meschaunce,
Than thoughe I had this woke ywonne a weye of Essex chese.
                          (ibid., 92-3)

[I'd be gladder, by God, to see Gilbert meet with misfortune
Than if I'd this week won a weight of Essex cheese.]

By the use of such a common, everyday idiom, enriched by the continuous use of familiar names which establish a real human setting for the Sins, Langland gives these scenes a ring of immediacy that enlivens relatively conventional types like Wrath. No strong emblematic features—except his "whyte eyen"—characterize the presentation of Anger. The whole effect depends on the unholy dispute between friars and parish-priests as to their rights in hearing confession; or, more evidently, on the fierce brawl between jealous nuns like "dame Johanne, dame Clarice and dame Peronelle", roused by the slanderous gossip of one whom Dante would classify as a sower of discord:

> "Of wykked wordes I, Wrath, here wortes i-made,
> Til 'thow lixte' and 'thow lixte' lopen oute at ones
> And eyther hitte other vnder the cheke;
> Hadde thei had knyues, bi Cryst her eyther had killed other."
> (ibid., 162-5)
> ["I, Wrath, prepared their vegetables with spiteful words,
> Until they leaped at once at each other with 'You lied!' and
> 'No, you did!';
> And they hit each other in the face;
> Had they knives, by Christ, each would have killed the
> other."]

The spirited squabbling and lively animosity of this scene resembles somehow the picture of the Wrathful in the IVth circle of the *Inferno;* but it cannot evidently compare with the destructive ferocity in which Dante has fixed for ever this particular aspect of evil—first in a group of anonymous sinners:

> Questi si percotean non pur con mano
>   ma con la testa e col petto e coi piedi
>   troncandosi co' denti a brano a brano.
> (*Inf.*, VII, 112-14)
> [They were smiting each other not only with the hand
> but with head and breast and feet and tearing
> each other piecemeal with their teeth.]

and later in the violent episode of Filippo Argenti (*Inf.*. VIII, 31-63). As regards Avarice and Gluttony it is again to the portraiture of the sin in *Inferno* that we must turn for the discovery of meaningful correspondences. The grotesque realism with which Langland depicts them has always been praised as an outstanding example of "character" literature. But more than being an early instance of the "types" of the naturalistic novel or an anticipation of Jonsonian "Humours",[24] these figures provide occasions for a sharp perception of human degradation. Prompted by a highly religious purpose, Langland as well as Dante see in these figures patterns of what we may call "insight allegory". The only difference, and a notable one in this case, is that whereas in the *Inferno* the full range of all possible manifestations of evil is displayed in varied but "distinct" series of images, the personifications of the Capital Sins in the *Visio* seem often to contain, gathered under one label, several of those aspects, through a skilful kind of human verisimilitude. This was evident in the case of Envy and Wrath: each had much of the other's character in his make-up. That is even truer of Avarice. His portrait proffers a rich association of significant details which deepen the essence of the besetting sin, and yet enlarge it in its many-sided relations; and this reminds us of similar revealing particulars in Dante's sinners. Avarice appears "hungriliche and holwe" (B, V, 189), but his beetling brows and thick, puffy lips resemble the swelling dropsy of the Falsifiers (*Inf.*, XXX, 52-5); his eyes are "blered as a blynde hagge" (line 191) and call to mind the squint-eyed Hoarders of the IVth circle (*Inf.*, VII, 40-1). I am perfectly aware that there is the risk here of straining the meaning of the lines or of treating their sense out of context.[25] But one cannot fail to see in Avarice's baggy cheeks, flapping around his chin "as a letheren

---

24. D. Traversi, "Piers Plowman" in *The Age of Chaucer* (Vol. I, *A Guide to Engl. Lit.*, ed. B. Ford), Pelican Book, p. 144.

25. This, I am afraid, happened to Mr. Bellezza in the course of his short comparative notes on the two poems, although I must admit that I am indebted to him for a few stimulating indications at this point of the present study. Cf. *Di Alcune Notevoli Coincidenze tra la D.C. e Pietro l'Aratore*, pp. 1224-28.

purs" (line 192), the suggestion of usury so eloquently indicated
by Dante in the shades of the Usurers:

> ... ma io m'accorsi
> che dal collo a ciascun pendea una tasca
> ch'avea certo colore e certo segno,
> e quindi pare che 'l loro occhio si pasca.
>
> (Inf., XVII, 54-7)
>
> [... but I observed
> that from the neck of each hung a pouch
> of a certain colour and device, and on
> these they seemed to feast their eyes.]

Again, when this grotesque creature is presented as clothed

> With an hode on his hed a lousi hatte aboue,
> And in a tauny tabarde of twelue wynter age ...
>
> (B, V, 195-6)
>
> [With a hood on his head, a lousy hat above,
> And in a tawny tabard of twelve winters' age ...]

we are given, graphically, the truth about the threadbare quality
of his trading activity.[26] Allegorically, this detail could moreover imply what is clearly evident later in the portrait—his
tendency to covert double-dealing. As such he calls to mind the

> cappe con cappucci bassi
> dinanzi agli occhi
> [cloaks with cowls down
> over their eyes]

which cover like a mask the Hypocrites of *Inf.*, XXIII (61-2), a
perfect expression of the simulation and expediency that charac-
terized them in life. Lest these impressions should seem too far-
fetched, it must be said that the accumulation of so many elements
in one personification opens out subsequently into a full development of each element, when, in the course of his confession,

---

26. Cf. Skeat, Vol. II, Notes, p. 82.

Avarice reveals himself not only as a covetous miser but, in succession, as a mean usurer, a falsifier, a thieving trickster, a hypocritical double-dealer (B, V, 200-62). Besides, the extensive account of his misdoings plunges us into the world of Malebolge, and seems to recreate the fraudulent atmosphere of the cantos of the Barrators (*Inf.*, XXI and XXII). The particular reference to "Coueytise" as a draper and moneylender has prompted a scholar with a flair for antiquarian research to discover in the "Sire Heruy" mentioned at the beginning of the episode a real person, William Hervy from Norfolk, merchant and public official, whose name is recorded in the Patent Rolls of the time.[27] Historical investigations of this kind are welcome in so far as they help to illuminate further the observational element in Langland's inspiration, and to strengthen the view that our poet, like Dante (though not as consistently as he), did not build his allegory "in vacuo" but drew instead, to a large extent, on the life he saw around him. But, of course, what finally counts is how effectively and truly the characters "live" in the poem; how successfully, that is, words, gestures, external features, internal attitudes, and appropriate environment translate and vivify the ideas of the author. Langland's vigorous delineation of Gluttony certainly obeys such criteria. The authentic setting of a smoky ale-house, the colloquial cast of speech, the noisy chorus of garrulous customers pouring the brew into Glotoun's craw, the disgusting vomiting of the undigested "gallons", all go to make a powerful scene of low comedy which can hardly be drawn merely in order to entertain, but is clearly meant to reveal the foul nature of the vice, the real condition of those "cuius deus venter est".

On the literal level Dante's illustration of this aspect of incontinence could not be more dissimilar. In sharp contrast with the rather extensive, if genuinely dramatic, picture of Langland, the references to Gluttony in the *Commedia* are quite "economical" and are not aimed at creating one or more scenes in which oustanding human figures would appear as Gluttony incarnate. On the sixth

27. M. E. Richardson, "Characters in Piers Plowman" in *Times Literary Supplement*, 13 January 1940, p. 24.

terrace of Purgatory, perhaps more than in any other parts of the cantica, it is the corrective purpose of the portrait of each aspect of the vice that is emphasized. The penitent Gluttonous are seen as a terribly emaciated crowd obliged to pass to and fro before a tall fruit-laden tree bedewed with clear water from a nearby spring, unable to satisfy their hunger or quench their thirst:

> Vidi gente sott'esso alzar le mani,
>   e gridar non so che verso le fronde,
>   quasi bramosi fantolin e vani,
> che pregano e 'l pregato non risponde
>   ma, per fare esser ben la voglia acuta,
>   tien alto lor disio e nol nasconde.
>
> (Purg., XXIV, 106-11)
> [I saw people beneath it lifting up their hands
> and crying I knew not what towards the foliage,
> like eager and thoughtless children who beg
> and he they beg of does not answer, but, to
> make their desire keener, holds up the thing
> they want and does not hide it.]

Voices from this tree proclaim examples of temperance; voices from another equally tantalizing tree declare examples of gluttony. Not all the shades are levelled to the anonymity of the group. Many, in fact, stand out in their individual humanity. But if these are "alive", they are so for other reasons than for their presentation as "types" of the sin.[28] Only a few are singled out as living images of Gluttony, although they are depicted with a touch of lightheartedness. Among the souls who are repenting by starvation their former excess in self-indulgence, we find for instance Pope Martin IV who

> purga per digiuno
> l'anguille di Bolsena e la vernaccia.
>
> (Purg., XXIV, 23-4)

28. Dante meets here e.g. Forese Donati, a former friend and kinsman. The encounter—one of the most touching of the poem—is the occasion for reviving old memories and recalling dear ones (XXIII, 40-133). Further on with Bonagiunta da Lucca Dante converses about poetry and the "sweet new style" (XXIV, 49-61).

> [purges by fasting
> the eels of Bolsena and the Vernaccia (wine).]

or messer Marchese degli Argogliosi,

> ch'ebbe spazio
> già di bere a Forlì con men secchezza,
> e sì fu tal che non si sentì sazio.
>
> (ibid., 31-3)[29]
>
> [who once had leisure
> for drinking at Forlì with less drought,
> yet was such that he never felt satisfied.]

And even in *Inferno,* the Florentine Ciacco "the hog" is introduced as a pitiful wretch rather than as a figure of monstrous appetite. Only by attending to the "contrapasso" of the turbid rain sluicing the ground, the putrid stench emanating from it, and by looking at the sinners wallowing in the mud under the fangs of the pot-bellied Cerberus (VII, 10-18), can we visualize the hideousness of the sin. "Gluton" moves in a comparable atmosphere of flatulent odours and belching sounds. The analogy between the two images can be drawn, therefore, not on the basis of any specific element of literal parallels, but rather by an assessment of the overall allegorical implications. Like Dante, Langland does not shrink from depicting the sheerly disgusting when this can reveal gross evil in a cogent manner. As Dante the traveller exclaims at a certain moment of his downward journey in Hell— when almost reluctantly he forces himself to look at some grotesque, even utterly repugnant manifestations of moral turpitude—

> ma nella chiesa
> coi santi, ed in taverna coi ghiottoni.
>
> (*Inf.,* XXII, 14-15)
>
> [but in church with
> saints and with guzzlers in the tavern.]

29. Benvenuto da Imola, one of the earliest commentators of the *Commedia,* noted, facetiously, that Pope Martin "plus tamen habuit curam anguillarum quam animarum"; to him also is due the anecdote about the Marchese's answer to a servant: "Domine, dicitur quod numquam facitis nisi bibere"; dixit ridenter: "Et quare numquam dicunt quod semper sitio?"; cf. Momigliano, op. cit., pp. 442-3.

For the English poet also, before man can be shown in the anxious pursuit of the challenging, yet rewarding, uplands of virtue, he must be shown as prone to wallow often in the morass of brute stupidity and near bestiality.

It is true that in the episode of the Confession of the Seven Deadly Sins, side by side with the satiric penetration with which he invests the description of various aspects of fallen nature, Langland shows a wholly humane understanding of man's feebleness, and recognizes the sincere impulse towards spiritual improvement. Nevertheless the resolve to rise again through repentance and forgiveness sounds, at this stage at least, rather perfunctory and does not blur the picture of the stark reality of sin. And Langland has represented it with such unbroken vigour of concrete imagination as to reveal himself as the possessor of an artistic perception which puts him nearer to Dante than any other poet of the Middle Ages. If then we want to find a formula expressing a significant similarity of imaginative process, we can suggest that if Dante's living characters precipitate, as it were, the moral and spiritual meaning of their symbolical function, Langland's personifications from a conventional abstractness attain to an equally valid incarnation of human truth. "The particular, the individual the concrete, the fleshed, the incarnate, is everywhere with the strength of reality and the irreducibility of reality itself. Here is vision truly made flesh." This remark, made some years ago by a distinguished critic in relation to the *Divine Comedy*,[30] can be referred, justifiably, to a considerable portion of the *Visio de Petro Plowman*. For both poets are most effective when they show good and evil substantially manifested in action and personality. Beyond and above every consideration of technique or formal rhetoric, it can be affirmed that the vivid representation of unregenerate and regenerate human nature is sustained by Dante throughout, but only partially, though certainly not less effectively, by the English poet.

To say this is to add to the stature of Langland. It must grow further.

30. C. S. Singleton, *Dante Studies,* I, Harvard University Press, 1954, p. 13.

CONCLUSION

The chief purpose of our study was to assess some possible thematic and artistic relationships between the major epic of Christian Medieval Literature and one of the most interesting poems produced in Europe by the same moral and spiritual vision of life.

Looking at Langland from a Dantesque perspective we have come to realize that, apart from differences in artistic refinement, in totality and lucidity of vision, and in structural integrity, *Piers Plowman,* in its central issues, deals with the same great subject matter as does the *Divine Comedy.* "The scene of *Piers Plowman",* H. W. Wells observed, "is precisely the opposite to that of Dante's poem. The Italian poet deals only with life beyond the grave, the English poet with life upon this side of the grave."[1] I trust I have shown that if the narrative, literal framework is different, and if the external setting conditions to a large extent the nature of the poetry in each work, the two poems, on the level of spiritual reality represented by the allegories, share in a fundamental vision of the human condition. The *Commedia* is Dante's contemporary life, his ethico-political life, represented in a crowd of personages and transferred into the other world. *Piers Plowman* is Langland's vision of his own time, grounded in the unalterable experience of human reality, but seen in a dream which points to infinite horizons. Allegory for both is the most effective means to search for the truth of man and God, the "device" used to state the same moral creed and to present the same religious vision.

Langland may lack many of the qualities which make Dante supreme, but—and this, I think, is our main conclusion—he has

1. *The Construction of Piers Plowman,* p. 129.

something his illustrious predecessor has not, or does not so consistently display. an immediate, thorough understanding of the simplicity and essentiality of the Gospel message. It seems strange, but Langland's practical attitude strives more insistently for the realization of the ideals of genuine Christianity—poverty and love. In stressing these aspects of the good life, one feels that, in a certain way, Langland completes Dante's vision from an ethico-religious point of view.

I do not pretend that this study is exhaustive. There is in the *Commedia* and *Piers* much more and much else than we have succeeded in examining in a short comparative analysis. And even if in many other important ways the two poems are irreducible to any comparative investigation, I do feel that there are other aspects which would offer a substantial, meaningful area of comparison. First, I am convinced that critics of *Piers Plowman* have not yet made up their minds as to what extent the experiences of its hero —the "Fool" or the "I" of the poem—are to be related to the experiences of the life and mind of its author. A study of this problem in the English poem in the light of its solution in the *Commedia* would, I feel, help greatly to illuminate this crucial aspect of Langland's work. Secondly, the relationship between Learning and the Good Life, a question central to both poems and one we have touched on rather summarily, would reveal significant connections, even if only to highlight the difference between the clear "scholastic" vision of the Italian poet and the more cloudy—yet dramatic and "dynamic"—experience of Langland. This would involve, for Dante, a reference to the *Convivio*. Just as one should depend, to a considerable extent, on Dante's *Monarchia* for a more extended study of both authors' "politics": another interesting topic which would yield some interesting results as far as fundamental ideas are concerned, in spite of the contrast between the universal theories of the Italian poet and the more limited "democratic" political views of the Englishman.

Further investigation of such common areas, developed on the lines which have guided us in our study, could—and should— extend one of the most interesting chapters of comparative Medieval Studies.

BIBLIOGRAPHY

So much has been written on Dante and Langland, particularly the former, that it has seemed advisable to give here only a select Bibliography of books and articles which have a direct bearing on this study.

(a) WORKS RELATING TO DANTE

(i) Texts and Commentaries

Le Opere di Dante Alighieri, a cura di E. Moore and P. Toynbee, Oxford, 1924.

La Divina Commedia, commentata da Attilio Momigliano, Firenze, 1948.

La Divina Commedia, a cura di Luigi Pietrobono, Torino, 1956.

The Comedy of Dante Alighieri, translated by D. L. Sayers (Penguin), *Hell,* 1953; *Purgatory,* 1955; *Paradise,* 1962 (with B. Reynolds).

(ii) Critical Studies

AUERBACH, E.: *Dante, Poet of the Secular World* (transl. R. Manheim), Chicago, 1961.

BATTAGLIA, S.: "Il Primo Verso del Poema Sacro" in *Il Veltro* (*Rivista della Civiltà Italiana*), Roma, 1961.

BRANDEIS, I.: *The Ladder of Vision, A Study of Dante's Comedy,* London, 1960.

BREGLIA, S.: *Poesia e Struttura nella Divina Commedia,* Genova, 1934.

COSMO, U.: *Guida a Dante,* Firenze, 1964.

CROCE, B.: *La Poesia di Dante,* Bari, 1948.

—— "Sul Concetto dell'Allegoria" in *Letteratura Italiana* (*Storia e Testi*), ed. Ricciardi, Napoli, 1951.

DUNBAR, H. F.: *Symbolism in Medieval Thought and its Consummation in the Divine Comedy*, New Haven, 1929.

ELIOT, T. S.: *Dante*, London, 1932.

FLETCHER, J. B.: *Dante*, London, 1916.

FERGUSSON, F.: *Dante*, London, 1963.

GETTO, G.: *Aspetti della Poesia di Dante*, Firenze, 1947.

GILBERT, A. H.: *Dante's Conception of Justice*, Durham. 1925.

GILSON, E.: *Dante the Philosopher* (transl. D. Moore), London, 1948.

MOMIGLIANO, A.: "Il Paesaggio nella Divina Commedia" in *Dante, Manzoni, Verga*, Messina, 1944.

MONTANO, R.: *Storia della Poesia di Dante*, Napoli, 1963.

NARDI, B.: *Dante e la Cultura Medievale*, Bari, 1949.

—— *Nel Mondo di Dante*, Roma, 1944.

—— *Il Punto sull'Epistola a Cangrande*, Firenze, 1960.

PAGLIARO, A.: "Simbolo e Allegoria nella Divina Commedia" in *L'Alighieri (Rassegna Bibliografica Dantesca)*, n. 2, 1963.

PASCOLI, G.: *Sotto il Velame*, Messina, 1900.

—— *La Mirabile Visione*, Messina, 1902.

PIETROBONO, L.: *La Struttura Morale della Commedia*, Torino, 1923.

RIZZO, T. L.: *Allegoria, Allegorismo e Poesia nella Divina Commedia*, Milano, 1941.

SANTI, G.: *L'Ordinamento Morale e l'Allegoria della Divina Commedia*, Palermo, 1923.

SAYERS, D. L.: *Introductory Papers on Dante*, London, 1954.

SCARTAZZINI, G.: *A Companion to Dante* (transl. A. J. Butler), London, 1893.

SINGLETON, C. S.: "Dante's Allegory" in *Speculum*, XXV, 1950.

—— "The Commedia: Elements of Structure" in *Dante's Studies*, I, Cambridge, Mass., 1954.

—— "Journey to Beatrice" in *Dante's Studies*, II, Cambridge, Mass., 1958.

SLATTERY, J. T.: *Dante*, New York, 1920.

STAMBLER, B.: *Dante's Other World—The Purgatorio as Guide to the Divine Comedy*, London, 1957.

WHITFIELD, J. H.: *Dante and Virgil*, Oxford, 1948.

(b) WORKS RELATING TO *PIERS PLOWMAN*

(i) Texts and Modernizations

"The Vision of William Concerning Piers Plowman" in *Three Parallel Texts*, ed. W. W. Skeat, Oxford, 1886 (two vols).
The Book Concerning Piers the Plowman, transl. into Modern English by D. and R. Attwater (Everyman), 1957.
Piers the Ploughman, A New Translation (Prose) by J. F. Goodridge (Penguin), 1959.

(ii) *Critical Studies*

ADAMS, J. F.: "Piers Plowman and the Three Ages of Man" in *J.E.G.Ph.*, LXI, January 1962.
BELLEZZA, P.: "Dante and Langland" in *Notes and Queries*, VIII, August 1894.
—— "Di Alcune Notevoli Coincidenze tra la Divina Commedia e Pietro l'Aratore" in *Rendiconti del Regio Instituto Lombardo di Scienze e Lettere*, II, XXIX, Milano, 1897.
BLOOMFIELD, M. W.: "The Present State of Piers Plowman Studies" in *Speculum*, XIV, April 1939.
—— *Piers Plowman as a Fourteenth Century Apocalypse*, Rutger Univ. Press, 1961.
BROOKE-ROSE, C.: "Ezra Pound: Piers Plowman in the Modern Waste Land" in *R.E.L.*, II, April 1961.
BURDACH, K.: *Der Dichter des Ackermann aus Böhmen und seine Zeit*, Berlin, 1932.
CHADWICK, D.: *Social Life in the Days of Piers Plowman*, Cambridge, 1922.
CHAMBERS, E. K.. "Long Will, Dante and the Righteous Heathen" in *Essays and Studies by Members of the Engl. Assoc.*, IX, Oxford, 1924.
—— *Man's Unconquerable Mind*, London, 1939.
COGHILL, N. K.: "The Character of P.P. Considered from the B Text" in *Med. Aevum*, II, 1933.
DAWSON, C. *Medieval Religion and Other Studies*, London, 1934.
DONALDSON, E. T.: *Piers Plowman, The C Text and its Poet*, New Haven, 1949.

DUNNING, T. P.: *Piers Plowman, An Interpretation of the A Text*, Dublin, 1937.

—— "The Structure of the B Text of P.P." in *R.E.S.*, VII, July 1956.

FOWLER, D. C.: *Piers Plowman—Literary Relations of A and B Texts*, Univ. of Washington Press, Seattle, 1961.

FRANK, R. W., Jr.: *Piers Plowman and the Scheme of Salvation*, New Haven, 1957.

—— "The Art of Reading Medieval Personification Allegory" in *E.L.H.*, XX, 1953.

GEROULD, G. H.: "The Structural Integrity of P.P." in *Studies in Philology*, XLV, January 1948.

HORT, G.: *Piers Plowman and Contemporary Religious Thought*, London, 1938.

HUSSEY, H.: "Langland, Hilton, and the Three Lives" in *R.E.S.*, VII, 1956.

JAMES, S. B.: *Back to Langland*, London, 1935.

JUSSERAND, J. J.: *Piers Plowman, A Contribution to the History of English Mysticism*, London, 1894.

KANE, G.: *Middle English Literature*, London, 1951.

LAWLOR, J.: "The Imaginative Unity of Piers Plowman" in *R.E.S.*, VIII, 1957.

—— *Piers Plowman. An Essay in Criticism*, London, 1962.

MERONEY, H.: "The Life and Death of Long Wille" in *E.L.H.*, XVII, 1950.

OWEN, D. L.: *Piers Plowman, A Comparison with some earlier contemporary French Allegories*, London, 1912.

RICHARDSON, M. E.: "Characters in Piers Plowman" in *Times Literary Supplement*, January 1940.

ROBERTSON, D. W., and HUPPE, B. F.: *Piers Plowman and Scriptural Tradition*, Princeton Univ. Press, 1951.

SALTER, E.: *Piers Plowman, An Introduction*, Oxford, 1962.

SMITH, A. H.: "Piers Plowman and the Pursuit of Poetry" (Inaugural Lecture at Univ. College, London), London, 1950.

SPEARING, A. C.: "The Art of Preaching and Piers Plowman" in *Criticism and Medieval Poetry*, London, 1964.

TRAVERSI, D.: "Langland's Piers Plowman" in *The Age of Chaucer* (Vol. I of *A Guide to English Literature*, ed. B. Ford), Penguin, 1955.

WELLS, H. W.: "The Construction of Piers Plowman" in *PMLA*, XLIV, 1929.

WOOLF, R.: "Some non Medieval Qualities of P.P." in *Essays in Criticism*, XII, April 1962.

(c) GENERAL

BALDINI, G.: *Storia della Letteratura Inglese*, Vol. I, Torino, 1958.

BAUGH, A. C. (ed.): *A Literary History of England*, I, London, 1950.

BLOOMFIELD, M. W.: *The Seven Deadly Sins*, Michigan, 1952.

BRINK TEN: *History of English Literature* (transl. H. M. Kennedy), Vol. I, London, 1895.

Cambridge History of English Literature, I and II.

COURTHOPE, W. J.: *A History of English Poetry*, I, London, 1895.

CURTIUS, E. R.: *European Literature and the Latin Middle Ages* (transl., W. R. Trask), London, 1953.

DE SANCTIS, F.: *Storia della Letteratura Italiana*, ed. Mondadori, Milano, 1961.

FLETCHER, A. S.: *Allegory, The Theory of a Symbolic Mode*, Cornell Univ. Press, New York, 1964.

FLORA, F.: *Storia della Letteratura Italiana*, Milano, 1947.

Letture Dantesche, a cura di G. Getto, Firenze, 1964.

GILSON, E.: *The Mystical Theology of St. Bernard* (transl. A. H. C. Downes), London, 1940.

HOUGH, G.: "The Allegorical Circle" in *Critical Quarterly*, Vol. 3, Autumn 1961.

HUIZINGA, J.: *The Waning of the Middle Ages* (transl.), London, 1924.

HUTTON, E.: *The Franciscans in England*, London, 1926.

LEGOUIS, E., and CAZAMIAN, L.: *A History of English Literature*, I, London, 1933.

LEWIS, C. S.: *The Allegory of Love*, Oxford, 1936.

McKISACK, M.: *The Fourteenth Century, Oxford History of England,* 1959.

MOORE, E.: *Studies in Dante,* Second Series, Oxford, 1903.

OWST, G. R.: *Preaching in Medieval England,* Cambridge, 1926.

—— *Literature and Pulpit in Medieval England,* Cambridge, 1933.

PANTIN, W. A.: *The English Church in the Fourteenth Century,* Cambridge, 1955.

PRAZ, M.: *Storia della Letteratura Inglese,* Firenze, 1937.

TILLYARD, E. M. W.: *The English Epic and its Background,* London, 1954.

INDEX